DERBY COUNTY
Miscellany

DERBY COUNTY
Miscellany

*Rams Trivia,
History, Facts & Stats*

PHIL MATTHEWS & GARETH DAVIS

DERBY COUNTY
Miscellany

Published By:
Pitch Publishing (Brighton) Ltd
A2 Yeoman Gate
Yeoman Way
Durrington
BN13 3QZ

Email: info@pitchpublishing.co.uk
Web: www.pitchpublishing.co.uk

First published 2011

13-digit ISBN: 978-1-9080510-7-3

Typesetting and origination by Pitch Publishing. Printed in India by Replika Press Pvt. Ltd. Manufacturing managed by Jellyfish Print Solutions Ltd.

FOREWORD BY MARC EDWORTHY

I was delighted to be invited to do the foreword for this book after all my memories of playing at Pride Park. I am sure you will find things that you never knew about your club in the following pages.

I had played for a number of big clubs before arriving at Pride Park – with Crystal Palace, Norwich City and Wolverhampton Wanderers amongst them – but none were any bigger than Derby County. Certainly, I played in no bigger game than the play-off final win over West Bromwich Albion.

I was born and raised in Devon, but my family and I made some good friends in the Derby area and there was never any doubt that we were going to settle down here when my playing days were over.

I was immediately impressed by both the size of the fanbase, and the passion of the supporters. They clearly love their football. Big crowds always made playing an experience to be savoured.

The club has a long and proud history and you quickly become aware of the triumphs enjoyed by Derby County over the years. They have regularly attracted quality players and there is no doubt that they deserve to be playing far higher up the table than they have managed for much of the last few years.

I would love to see the club back playing in the Premier League, and although it is a big ask for any club to get there these days, the likes of Blackpool show it can still be done.

ACKNOWLEDGEMENTS

The authors would like to acknowledge the following sources for their assistance in the writing of this book: *The Derby Telegraph*, *Derby County the Complete Record* by Gerald Mortimer, *The Little Book of Derby County* by Peter Seddon, *There Was Some Football Too* by Tony Francis; Mike Wilson, David Moore, Andy Ellis, and the staff and supporters of Derby County for their help and ideas.

INTRODUCTION

There's an oft-used phrase that goes 'it can only happen at Derby County' and when you look back at the history of a football club that has been in existence for over 125 years, you can see plenty of truth in those few words.

How many other clubs, for example, could have a chairman turn up for a game in a helicopter and leave the ground thinking supporters were waving to him when in fact they were raising two fingers in his direction?

And can you name another club that would win the Football League and then let the victorious manager go within 18 months – not once, but twice, and both in the space of a few years?

Derby County Miscellany makes no claim to be the definitive record of all things bright and beautiful to do with the club, or all things weird and wonderful, but by the time you have reached the end we are sure you will know far more about your favourite club than you did previously.

The book also features the Rams' leading ten appearance-makers, charting their careers and some of the stranger aspects of their time with the club, along with ten of the most memorable home fixtures covering some classics from the Baseball Ground and Pride Park Stadium.

As lifelong Rams fans, authors Phil Matthews and Gareth Davis have both found writing this book an absolute pleasure and hope that you, the supporters, enjoy reading it just as much. Because when everything is taken into account, the fans of a club are the ones who matter most – and Derby County certainly has some of the best support around.

Come on you Rams!

Phil Matthews and Gareth Davis

IN THE BEGINNING

It was a need to generate extra funds for the cricket club that brought Derby County into being. The first Derbyshire Cup final was played at the County Ground in front of a crowd of approximately 7,000. The prospect of filling the coffers, allied to a way to keep players and spectators interested in the club during winter time, made the prospect irresistible.

BLOOMIN' ECONOMY

The economic situation in the West Midlands was directly responsible for the Rams signing their greatest-ever player. Steve Bloomer was born in Cradley but his father's search for work brought him to Derby as a youngster. Growing up in the town and with a talent for football Steve quickly established himself in the team.

ODDEST FIRST

There is little doubt that even for a club that chalked up a number of firsts, the oddest one belonged to Jack Howe. Howe, a normally dependable full-back, had started having judgement issues when heading the ball. A diagnosed sight defect led to Howe becoming the first player in the country to play in contact lenses. Howe went one better when making his debut for England against Italy, becoming the first England international to play wearing them.

DIFFERENT STROKES

It may sound like a joke, but in the early days of professional football the Rams had two brothers playing for them with the surname Goodall. Nothing odd in that you might say, but the pair, who both became full internationals, actually played for different countries. Archie was capped for Ireland, while brother John featured for England. The pair were also totally different in temperament, with Archie a firebrand and John a gentleman.

A CONTRACT IS A CONTRACT

Archie Goodall was arguably the first player to carry out his own form of industrial action while playing in the 1894 United Counties league cup final. The result was still undecided at the end of 90 minutes, and the rules dictated, therefore, that extra-time would be played. Goodall decided, however, that his contract only stipulated that he played the 90 minutes. As a result he simply refused to play extra-time – leaving his team-mates a man short.

FROM DISTANT SHORES

Tewfik Abdallah has his own unique place in Rams history for being the first overseas player to feature in a Derby shirt. Abdallah was not scouted from abroad, but turned up at the Baseball Ground uninvited. His lack of command of the English language meant that the only three words he could speak on arrival were "foot the ball". After managing to convince the club that he wanted to play for them and not buy a season ticket, he made 15 appearances in 1920/21.

INVISIBLE SPONSORSHIP

The Rams were the first club in the 92-strong Football League (in the days before the Premier League) to have their shirts sponsored. Swedish motorcar manufacturers Saab were the sponsors and the brand name was emblazoned in big red letters across the front of the shirts in time for the 1978/79 pre-season photographs. Senior players were also given Saab cars to drive. Unfortunately, the Football League did not have the wit or wisdom to condone the idea and the club had to play in plain white shirts for all competitive fixtures that season.

WHAT'S IN A NAME?

The Rams have always been called Derby County FC, but that was not the original intention. When first formed as a winter offshoot of Derbyshire County Cricket Club, the plan was to name the football side Derbyshire County Football Club, but this idea was quashed by the County FA who felt the name was too long, thus allowing for the creation of the shorter Derby County FC.

JUST LIKE WATCHING ENGLAND

Many clubs have supporters who chant, when playing well, that it is just like watching Brazil. Brian Clough took the idea further, changing the traditional black shorts and white shirts to the same blue hue worn by England, along with red numbers which were also sported by the national side. His logic was that if his teams ran out dressed like England they would feel that they were England and perform to their absolute maximum. It's not known how the Welsh and especially, Scottish members of the squad took to the idea, although the club enjoyed its most successful years while wearing this colour scheme.

TOP TEN APPEARANCES – 10. STEVE POWELL

Steve Powell made his first-team debut at the age of 16 years and 30 days, in a Texaco Cup match early in the 1971/72 season under Brian Clough. His league debut came three days later in a 2-1 victory over Arsenal in the early days of the Rams' journey to their first-ever championship title. But Steve is also very much remembered for his outing in the game that ultimately clinched the title at the end of the campaign. Still 16, Steve was thrown in by Clough for a crucial fixture at home to Liverpool, Derby's last game of the season, and gave a mature performance in a 1-0 win that eventually saw the title come to the Baseball Ground. Derby-born and a pupil at Bemrose School, Steve came through the club's ranks to follow in the footsteps of his dad Tommy and gave exceptional service to the Rams. Steve made 420 appearances overall and between them the Powells played over 800 senior games. There was a third generation of Powell, Steve's son, also called Steve, who was in the youth system in the 1990s but unfortunately didn't make it as a professional. Steve senior played 15 games as Derby won the Football League again under Dave Mackay in 1974/75 and was comfortable either as a defender, where he had made his early appearances, or a midfielder. Such was his popularity and consistency that he was named as the supporters' Player of the Year in the 1978/79 season. A loyal servant, Steve remained a part of the furniture at the Baseball Ground for 14 years; from his debut in 1971 to his final match in 1985. He played in three divisions for the club, having made his debut in Division One, then in the sides that were also in Division Two, and then Division Three, after two relegations. Steve played under eight managers in his time as a regular at Derby – Clough, Mackay, Colin Murphy, Tommy Docherty, Colin Addison, John Newman, Peter Taylor and Arthur Cox – and all regarded him as an important member of their squad. After retiring, Steve later managed Burton Albion, then a non-league side, and went on to work at Derby College. The surname Powell is actually one of the most common to appear for the Rams with seven having turned out over the years – Ken, Tommy, Steve, Barry, Chris, Darryl and Darren – although only Tommy and Steve are related.

CHANGE OF DIRECTION

There are those who, throughout Derby County's 127-year history, may claim that the team did not know whether it was coming or going. While that is debatable it is certainly a criticism that can be claimed fairly against the official club crest. For the majority of time since the first badge was adopted in 1924 a ram's head, and more recently an outline of the whole animal, has faced left. However, on more than one occasion revamps have shown the creature facing the other way. The first time it was reversed in 1981 the club ended up falling into the Third Division. It was restored to its favoured direction after 12 years. Direction was again changed in 1995, but restored to face left once again two years later and has remained that way ever since.

TRUE COLOURS

If you ask most football supporters what colour strip the Rams play in the majority would answer 'white shirts and black shorts'. For much of the club's history that would be correct, but they have had a number of different-coloured first-choice strips over the years. The very first adopted the colours of Derbyshire Cricket Club, with blue sleeves, amber and brown shirts and white shorts. The following year saw them change to black shorts, and blue shirts with red sleeves, before the following year changing the multi-coloured shirt for a white one with a red pocket. Ignoring the annual tinkering with styles that all clubs seem to do in order to sell more replica kits, Derby has had 12 different-colour makeovers of their strip. Several times they have had black and white striped tops and most garishly a red, black, and white striped shirt for the 1894/95 season.

THE TEAM AT PLATFORM ONE

Derby County can thank the railway industry for their very existence. It was a Midland Railway clerk by the name of William Morley who first came up with the idea of forming the team. He discussed the idea with his father, who was also called William and who just happened to be a committee member of Derbyshire County Cricket club. It was William senior who proposed the idea to the committee, and the rest, as they say, is history.

HEROES AND VILLAINS

One of, if not the, defining moments in the history of the club came before the formation of the Football League on Saturday 14th November 1885. The Rams were drawn against Aston Villa in the second round of the FA Cup. Villa were already considered a big name in the game, but ended up losing 2-0. Even though the match was played at Derby the team had clearly arrived.

FIRST IS WORSE

Over the years the Rams have faced many of the biggest clubs in the game, both domestically and abroad. Teams such as Real Madrid, Juventus, and Benfica have come up against Derby County in competitive fixtures, and in several cases have been well and truly beaten. Derby's first competitive match was against much less exalted opposition and was also without a happy outcome. They lost 7-0 at home to Walsall Town in the FA Cup.

EIGHT TRUE GREATS

When the Football League celebrated its 100th anniversary one of the ways of marking the occasion was to draw up a list of the 100 greatest players, entitled '100 legendary football players'. Eight of those on the list had played for Derby. The eight were; John Goodall, Steve Bloomer, Hughie Gallacher, Raich Carter, Peter Doherty, Dave McKay, Peter Shilton, and Paul McGrath.

NO PLACE LIKE HOME

Football may be 'the world game' but Derby County has yet to look outside the British Isles when it comes to appointing a manager. There have been 26 bosses to date (not including caretakers) since Harry Newbould became the first to officially hold the title in 1896. All have been English apart from five who came from Scotland.

FIRST AMONGST EQUALS

It is difficult to decide what exactly is considered success for a football manager, but if winning promotion at your first attempt is any indicator then Derby County has just three candidates in its history. The trio is George Jobey in the 1925/26 season, Jim Smith in 1995/96, and Billy Davies in 2006/07.

TEN GREAT HOME MATCHES – DERBY 5 ARSENAL 0

One of the greatest sides of the first half of the 1970s was Arsenal. They were the first club of the modern age to complete the league and cup double of FA Cup winners and Division One champions. Any meeting between the two clubs was eagerly anticipated. Even by the lofty standards set previously, the game at the Baseball Ground on November 25th 1972 was a little bit special. Derby dominated the tie almost from first to last, and Alan Hinton proved particularly troublesome for the Gunners defence with assists for three of the goals and a trademark rasping strike for one of his own. The 5-0 demolition of the visitors took place in no more than 26 minutes with four of the goals coming during a particularly fruitful ten-minute spell. Hinton was certainly the creator of the goals but heroes were to be found all over the park. Derby had no less than six full internationals in their side, and two had reached Under-23 level. Charlie George tried his luck in the opening stages with the tie goalless but provided Derby keeper Colin Boulton with little to worry about. The hosts proved so dominant that they had rattled in all five goals before Boulton was called in to real action again. John McGovern started the goal-fest with a goal on 21 minutes after the experienced Bob Wilson – freshly back from a lengthy injury lay-off – in the Arsenal goal failed to deal with an Archie Gemmill cross. The Rams were denied a legitimate second after a Hinton free kick was deemed to be taken too quickly for the liking of the referee. It only served to motivate Hinton who doubled the lead on 37 minutes with a rocket shot. Roy McFarland was next to score – heading another Hinton cross home three minutes later. With two minutes more played the Rams were out of sight of their opponents as again Hinton provided another peerless pass, this time allowing Kevin Hector to nod a free kick past Wilson. If Arsenal thought that the half-time break had allowed them to regroup it only took two minutes of the second period to convince them otherwise. Yet again the ammunition was provided by Hinton. This time it was a first Rams goal for Roger Davies. There was no further scoring but second-in-the-table Arsenal ended the day decidedly second best. Final score: Derby 5-0 Arsenal.

MANAGING BY NUMBERS

The managerial statistics are always an interesting point in a club's history. Did you know, for example, that while he isn't widely regarded as a successful Derby County boss, Roy McFarland has a win percentage right up there among the best? Or that Colin Murphy, who departed the hotseat in 1977, was only the third manager in almost a century to leave his position having taken charge of less than 100 games? George Jobey has the honour of having led Derby in more matches than anyone else, his 629 coming from August 1925 to May 1941 and including promotion at the first attempt plus two top-flight runner-up spots. Behind Jobey is Jimmy Methven, the second full-time boss in Derby's history, who followed over 500 games for the club as a player with 498 as the gaffer after taking over from Harry Newbould. Newbould led the club from 1896, 12 years after the club's formation – in the early days the team was selected by committee – and took charge of 376 games. But the third-longest man in charge is Arthur Cox, who led the club on 453 occasions, before standing down due to a back problem in October 1993. Brian Clough and Jim Smith managed 289 and 281 games, respectively, while Harry Storer (332) and Stuart McMillan (346) are the only others to top 300. By the end of 2010/11, Nigel Clough had taken charge of 122 fixtures, ranking him 12th on the all-time list. In terms of win percentages, putting aside caretaker managers (David Lowe and Chris Hutchings, in 2009, both won their sole games), the best record is that of Ted Magner with nine wins from 11 – for 81.82 per cent – in 1945. Of those to have been in charge at the Baseball Ground for a significant length of time, however, the leading figure is provided by Brian Clough, whose 289 games in the hotseat in all competitions realised 135 wins for a percentage of 46.71. Cecil Potter has the next-best total of 45.26 with 62 wins from his 137 matches between July 1922 and July 1935.

Billy Davies comes in next at 44.93 for his spell, although having taken Derby to the Premier League in 2007 he then won just one top-flight fixture, otherwise his record could have been higher. Nigel Clough's win percentage stands at 30.33, while at the other end of the scale the highest percentage of losses is held by Colin Todd, with 11 defeats in 17 fixtures for 64.71 per cent.

RECORD WIN

For many years the Rams could boast a record score in a competitive fixture – a 12-0 victory over Finn Harps on September 15th 1976 in the Uefa Cup. However, even this incredible score was eclipsed on January 5th 2011 when the Rams were drawn at home against Shirebrook Town in the Derbyshire Senior Cup. The original plan was that Derby County would treat the tournament as additional reserve team fixtures in order to give extra experience or game time to youngsters and squad members, but there were so many players returning to fitness or struggling for form that nine of the starting XI could consider themselves genuine first-team squad members. Shirebrook took a very early lead but then conceded 14 without reply to end up on the wrong end of a 14-1 scoreline, a figure that is unlikely ever to be beaten.

HOME HIGHS

Derby County was a club regularly contesting the latter stages of the FA Cup around the turn of the 20th century, but never managed to pick up the trophy. They did, however, enter the record books in 1903 thanks to a poor piece of selection. Regular goalkeeper Jack Fryer had been injured in a game on Easter Monday, and though clearly not having recovered sufficiently, was chosen to play in the final. In the days before substitutes were allowed Fryer took turns with Jimmy Methven and Charlie Morris between the posts, with newspapers describing matters as "a fiasco". Regardless of who made the decision to let Fryer play, cup final opponents Bury scored six unanswered goals marking April 18th 1903 in the record books as the highest FA Cup Final defeat in history.

SICK OF THE SIGHT

Leeds City must have been sick of the sight of Alf Bentley. Not only did he score past them in two consecutive seasons, he hit four on each occasion.

IMPRESSIVE

In his first full season with the Rams, Alf Bentley scored four goals on two separate occasions. He hit all four in the win over Barnsley and was one of three strikers in the 6-1 victory against Leeds City. Thomas Dilly and Edward Garry hit the other two.

TOTAL OPPOSITES

There have been a number of brothers with Rams connections throughout Derby County's history. Take Archie and John Goodall for example; while John was always referred to as 'Gentleman John' because of his temperament and character, Archie was a far fierier individual who, as mentioned elsewhere in this book, actually refused to play extra-time in a game because he said his contract was for the initial 90 minutes.

IGNORE ME I'M LOCAL

If the Player of the Year trophy is anything to go by then the argument that locally produced players are never appreciated as much as those brought in from outside is definitely true. Only six times out of 42 has the winner come up through the ranks.

BAD DAY AT THE OFFICE

If you accept the highs there is little doubt you must also be prepared to take the lows, and for the Rams one of the lowest moments in their history came on January 18th 1900. Derby County were drawn away to Everton in the FA Cup and despite putting two goals past the home side were comprehensively beaten 11-2.

BETTER THAN THIS

The phrase 'things can only get better' may not have been written specifically about Derby County but it certainly should have been after their first game against Great Lever. The Lancashire club completely outplayed the Rams, winning by a whopping 6-0. The date was September 13th 1884. Great Lever did not exist for long but deserve a mention in Derby history not only for this result but also for bringing one of the all-time Rams greats into the English game – John Goodall.

UP TO THE PLATE

Like many sportsmen Steve Bloomer found himself gifted in more than one sport. Footballers who also played cricket were fairly common, and Bloomer did indeed play cricket at an amateur level, but it was at baseball that the Derby striker excelled. Steve was a member of Derby County Baseball Club and was part of the side that became British champions on three separate occasions in the 1890s.

THREE HOMES FOR ENGLAND

Many football clubs have moved home over the years, and Derby County cannot even claim to be the only club to move more than once. They do however boast the proud, and unique, record of being the only one to have hosted full internationals in all three of them. The County Ground was the venue when England beat Ireland 9-0. The same two sides met at the Baseball Ground with a 2-1 victory for England, while Pride Park was the scene for a 4-0 victory by England over Mexico.

BAT AND BALL CLASH

The Rams have only had three homes since their formation in 1884. As the club was originally formed to give members of the cricket club something to do in the winter months, they initially played at the County Cricket Ground, or the Racecourse as it is often known. Even in an age when football and cricket were considered winter and summer sports, respectively, there was the occasional fixture clash. As a result the footballers moved out and took up residence at Sir Francis Ley's Baseball Ground on a permanent basis in 1895 after a couple of previous 'one-offs'. They stayed there until 1997 when they moved to the brand new, purpose built, Pride Park.

LEY'S PITCH

Most fans know that Derby County played their football for many a year at the Baseball Ground, but are not always sure why the stadium was so called. It all came about because of Sir Francis Ley. Ley owned a company named Ley's Malleable Castings. On a trip to America he was extremely impressed to discover a number of companies provided a field laid out for baseball as a way of providing both recreation and physical exercise for employees. He decided to do the same on his return to Derby. The National Baseball League of Great Britain and Ireland was formed in 1890 and Ley's side ran away with the first championship. The team included the legendary Steve Bloomer, amongst others. The baseball club lasted until 1898 after which time it was used exclusively for football. Ironically, much criticism was thrown at the baseball team for importing too many foreign players (American). How many times have we heard that in professional sport over the years?

SON OF YOUR FATHER

The name Clough is one that has been synonymous with Derby County ever since Brian first arrived in 1967. Although not immediately successful, he arrived like a whirlwind and things were never the same after. With his family being brought up in the area, and son Nigel moving into management after a successful playing career, it was always wondered by fans whether he would follow his dad to either of the two clubs he had most of his success at, Derby and Nottingham Forest. January 2009 gave the answer when Nigel was unveiled as the replacement for Paul Jewell. The official announcement came on the evening that Derby County played their Carling Cup semi-final first leg at home to Manchester United. The 1-0 win for the Rams suggested that Clough junior had the magic formula. His brief, though, was to drastically reduce the wage bill and move many of the bigger-named players on to pastures new rather than immediately build a side geared towards promotion.

LIKE FATHER

The Powell family was one with Derby County coursing through its veins. Tommy Powell was the first to gain recognition in a Derby shirt, making his debut as a 16-year-old on Christmas Day 1941. A talented and tricky winger, he served the club until finally hanging up his boots in 1962. Son Steve had no such problem coming through the ranks just as Brian Clough was making the club the pre-eminent side in England. Although making his debut in a Texaco Cup match, most people would remember him for his display against Liverpool in the last match of the campaign which ultimately won the club the league championship for the first time in its history. Steve made 409 starts and 11 substitute appearances, and would probably have made even more but for injury. His son Steve junior was also on the books at the club but never managed to break through to the senior side.

TEN FROM TWELVE

Derby County were invited to become one of the founder members when the Football League was formed in 1888. As both Accrington Stanley and Stoke dropped out over the years only for the names to reappear later, the Rams are one of only ten teams to play every single season since its formation.

NIGEL CLOUGH ON THE DAY HE WAS APPOINTED DERBY BOSS

THE BROTHERS BLOOMER

One played a solitary game in Derby colours, while his brother went on to become the greatest player in Derby history. They were the Bloomer brothers. Steve was the elder of the two and his total of 291 league goals in 473 games is a club record that is unlikely to ever be beaten, and his total of 317 goals in 536 First Division games for the Rams and Middlesbrough is a record only beaten by Jimmy Greaves so far. Steve's brother Philip was a left-back. He played just once for Derby before dying of peritonitis at the tragically young age of 21.

WHAT A START

Derby County had an incredible start to their first Football League campaign. Drawn away to Bolton Wanderers they found themselves 3-0 down, before mounting a spirited comeback to win the match 6-3.

TWICE AS NICE

Apart from both being English, and both defenders, Steve Buckley and Mark Wright had very little in common, other than being the only two players in the 42-year history of the Player of the Year Trophy, or Jack Stamps Trophy to give it the proper name, to have won it twice. Given the illustrious names to appear on that roll of honour once, twice is something very special.

STEVE BLOOMER'S WATCHING

Steve Bloomer is watching according to the words of the song, and in a way he truly is. A bust of Bloomer mounted on brickwork, from the Baseball Ground, was unveiled on January 17th 2009, before the start of the home match at Pride Park against Queens Park Rangers. The bust is believed to be the first one at pitch-side anywhere in the country.

FIFTY NOT OUT

In any line of business to have worked for the same organisation for 50 years is something pretty special, and therefore there were no dissenting voices when Gordon Guthrie was awarded an MBE for serving Derby County for such a period. Guthrie had started as a reserve-team player and served under no less than 23 different managers in his time at the club.

TOP TEN APPEARANCES – 9. ARCHIE GOODALL

Archie Goodall was one of Derby County's first true great players, and indeed one of the first great names of the English game. He was born in Belfast but played initially for Preston North End before moving to Aston Villa in 1888, and then Derby a year later. Archie served as the Rams club captain during his time at the club as he helped establish them as a team capable of challenging for the top honours. He helped Derby finish as runners-up in the Football League in 1896 and also helped the club to three FA Cup finals. Ahead of the 1898 final against Nottingham Forest, Archie was caught trying to off-load his allocated tickets to a ticket tout and although Derby were strong favourites, they lost 3-1. They were back for the final a year later, although Archie missed out through injury, and went down 4-1 to Sheffield United, then in 1903 Archie was the skipper as the Rams were beaten 6-0 by Bury in what remains a record FA Cup final scoreline. Controversy was never far away from Archie as, alongside the ticket tout incident, in 1894 he refused to play extra-time in a United Counties League Cup final against West Bromwich Albion, citing his contract, which only covered 90-minute matches. But as a centre-half he was a mightily effective player due to his strength, stamina and physical presence, which also meant he could play in midfield if required. Archie made a club-record 151 consecutive appearances between October 1892 and 1897 and overall played 423 times for the Rams. He played at Preston North End with his brother John, who he was reunited with at Derby, and the pair is unique for being the first brothers to play international football for different countries. They were raised in Scotland, to Scottish parents, but because of their birthplaces were not able to play for Scotland, so Archie became an Ireland cap – in those days there was no major split between north and south – while London-born John played for England. While with Derby, Archie made his debut for Ireland and soon became the oldest player to score in international football during the 19th century. After leaving the Rams he played briefly for Plymouth Argyle, became player-manager at Glossop North End, and then signed for Wolverhampton Wanderers, becoming Wolves' oldest-ever player. Upon his retirement as a player, Archie travelled Europe and the United States as part of a strongman act before settling in London, where he died aged 65 in 1923.

BUCK IN THE PARK

Known as the Rams almost from time immemorial, the club would more aptly have been named the Stags or the Bucks, as the town crest features a deer. Early club crests included the deer as part of the badge. The local army regiment – the Sherwood Foresters – had a ram as a mascot and the football club adopted it.

HERO TO ZERO (1)

George Jobey served Derby County as manager from 1925 until 1941. He is in an elite group of bosses who have taken the Rams to promotion at the first time of asking. Jobey managed far more than that, though, leading his players to the runners-up spot twice. Sadly, Jobey is more likely to be remembered for being given a lifetime ban from the game in 1941 for offering players illegal inducements to sign for Derby County. The ban was lifted four years later.

DEFENCE ON TOP

The Player of the Year trophy was introduced in 1969. Out of the 42 years that the award has been in operation, defenders have come out on top 24 times, with Roy McFarland the first winner and John Brayford the most recent in 2011 – at time of writing. Whether the balance falls the way of those who attempt to prevent goals is down to the number of campaigns that the Rams have been battling against relegation is not proven, but likely. The 2007/08 season proved to be so poor that the fans were encouraged to give it to themselves, and indeed did so.

THE FIRST MANAGER

For the first 16 years of existence as a league club, the Derby County team was selected by a committee. On becoming a limited company in 1896, Mr W D Clark was named as manager, but it was in 1900 that Harry Newbould not only inherited the title but also the role that people would recognise as football-team manager. In July 1906, Newbould moved to Manchester City to take over a similar role. The decision was made at least partly because of the Rams' decision to sell Steve Bloomer to Middlesbrough – a decision that Newbould definitely did not approve of.

NEVER A BORROWER BE

When Derby County turned up at the Anfield Road ground that Everton used to play at they had only ten players. Incredibly, they managed to persuade their opponents to lend them one of theirs in order to have a full side. The player they used was called Harry Harbour, who played for the reserve team. It must have been a bittersweet occasion for Harbour whose parent club won 6-2.

BY ROYAL APPOINTMENT

When Her Majesty the Queen and the Duke of Edinburgh formally opened Pride Park Stadium on July 18th 1997 it was a very proud day for the club, made even more so by the fact that this was the first time that the Queen had officiated at the opening of a football ground.

OFF THE PEG?

Many supporters claim that Pride Park looks very similar to Middlesbrough's Riverside Stadium, and there is a very good reason for that. When the Derby County board of directors made the decision to build a brand new stadium they visited a number of other new grounds and decided that with a few adaptations the Riverside was the closest to what they wanted.

BY ROYAL APPOINTMENT AGAIN

Her Majesty the Queen may not be a Derby County season-ticket holder but she has made more official visits to Pride Park than any other league ground during her reign. Having formally opened the new ground in 1997 the stadium was chosen as the venue for the Derby stage of her Golden Jubilee celebrations. The date chosen was August 1st 2002.

MEE WHO?

You would have to search hard to find the name Bertie Mee in Derby County records. He played for the reserves but never made a senior appearance. After moving on, injury curtailed his career, and he trained to be a physiotherapist at one of the local hospitals. Mee was then invited to replace the outgoing physio and was then asked to replace Billy Wright as manager. He went on to become the first manager in modern times to win the Football League and FA Cup double.

SLIPPED DISC

Derby County fans are famed for their singing efforts from the terraces – but have you heard the full album of tracks all about the club? It's called The Rams' Songs and has been out for several years but remains available on CD and also in digital formats. The Rams' Songs contains 14 individual tracks covering the great and the good of Derby's history. Club anthem Steve Bloomer's Watching kicks it all off but what follows is a collection of songs, tales, mixes and more that can best be described as eclectic. The Dam Busters March is on there sandwiched between a track called The Derby Rams – a folk-based effort – and one called You Can't Win Them All, a song that also carries a heart-warming message about protecting the beautiful game by Brian Clough. The Rams' Songs warrants a place in any Derby fan's collection, as much for the random nature of the collection as the quality of songs!

KEEPING YOUR PLACE

Stability is key to the chances of any team's successes, particularly with a reliable and regular goalkeeper as your last line of defence. A couple of times in recent seasons the Rams have fielded four different stoppers across the campaign, but in 2010/11 they went one further and used five in Championship fixtures. Stephen Bywater started the campaign as number one but picked up an injury in the autumn, leading to the loan signing of Frank Fielding from Blackburn Rovers. Goalkeeper number three was teenage Academy product James Severn, as a substitute in the home defeat to Hull City when Bywater had gone off injured. Fielding returned but was only able to play a handful of games under emergency loan terms, so the Rams later took on Brad Jones from Liverpool. Australian international Jones was hardly a massive hit and on the final day Derby used their fifth keeper, Ross Atkins, who was given his senior debut after coming through the Academy. And you can add a couple of keepers who were on the bench but never made it on to the pitch. Saul Deeney was Bywater's regular backup but their injuries coincided, then Matt Duke arrived on loan from Hull City and would have replaced Fielding in April but was called back, so Jones came in.

TEN GREAT HOME MATCHES – DERBY 4 REAL MADRID 1

It is frequently described as the greatest match in the Rams' history. Real Madrid have always been one of the great sides in European football and the 1975/76 season paired them with an in-form Derby County side with this, the first leg, at home. Big names had already visited the Baseball Ground in European tournaments but were not necessarily at the peak of their powers at the time. Real were a different animal altogether though. The *Derby Evening Telegraph* declared Derby good enough to go all the way to the final on the back of this match-winning display. There was little doubt that Rams fans had seen their team utterly dominate proceedings for much of the night. The Rams were ahead as early as the tenth minute with a team goal of great skill. Colin Todd played his pass from a throw-in across the pitch to David Nish who took the ball on before feeding Archie Gemmill. The Scot struck a low ball into the box which Charlie George fired viciously into the net with his left foot. It is a goal still talked of nowadays as one of the greatest ever seen at the Baseball Ground. Seven minutes later the Rams were two goals to the good. Francis Lee went down in the box, a little too easily for the Spanish side, and the referee pointed to the spot despite protestations. George took the spot-kick, this time with his right, and with a shot that was too much for the keeper to deal with. Madrid pulled themselves back into the tie when Pirri, the Spain captain, beat the offside trap to make the score 2-1. Derby restored their two-goal advantage two minutes before half-time when Nish fired in a low drive from the edge of the box that the keeper should really have done better with. Real came out for the second-half determined to reduce the deficit, and would have done so but for a linesman ruling out what looked to be a perfectly valid goal for a dubious offside call. With 78 minutes on the clock, Real must have thought that the officials were conspiring against them as a second penalty was awarded, this time for a foul on Kevin Hector. Once more the Spanish outfit thought that any contact was minimal, and once again up stepped George to score from the spot. The Derby man had his hat-trick and the Rams won 4-1.

THE FIRST TWELVE

The Rams were one of 12 teams who formed the Football League in its first season in 1888. The full list is: Accrington, Aston Villa, Blackburn Rovers, Bolton Wanderers, Burnley, Derby County, Everton, Notts County, Preston North End, Stoke, West Bromwich Albion and Wolverhampton Wanderers.

JUST ONE CHANCE

The Rams' first league campaign may have only consisted of 22 matches but the club still managed to use 29 different players in total. This included eight with just one appearance each.

CALL ME NUMBER ONE

The first goalscoring hero for the Rams was Sandy Higgins. He scored 11 league goals, and 12 altogether, in the club's first league season. This was more than a quarter of Derby's entire league tally.

ALL OF A TISWAS

It is unlikely that David Nish and Roger Davies ever thought that their footballing success would lead to an appearance on primetime children's television on the wrong end of a custard pie attack. Nish and Davies, however, found themselves on cult TV show *Tiswas* being attacked by the notorious Phantom Flan Flinger. The reason for the invite was that co-presenter Trevor East was a huge Rams fan.

BOARD MEETING

Football-led celebrity merchandising is not something freshly introduced by David Beckham and players of his era. Derby County players Roger Davies and David Nish marketed a board game in the mid-1970s called Top Club Soccer. The game was likened to Monopoly with a football slant.

I'M THE GREATEST

Franz Beckenbauer, Johann Cruyff, Carlos Alberto, Roger Davies. Which of those was the greatest player? According to the Americans the answer is Davies. In the days when players signed up for the American Major League Soccer at the end of their careers, Davies was voted the MVP – or most valuable player in the league by his peers – beating the other three to the top honour. His trophy was presented by Sylvester Stallone.

FOUR SURE

The name of Sandy Higgins should go down in Derby history as the first player to score four goals in a game. The most scored by any individual in a single match previously had been two. For the record, Higgins' personal triumph came on March 9th 1889 in the 5-2 home win against Aston Villa.

BUNYAN'S PROGRESS

The 1890/91 season was a defensive disaster for the Rams. They conceded 81 goals, which was 18 more than anyone else. Deciding on a change of keeper towards the end of the season, curiously they chose to bring in Charles Bunyan, a goalie who had conceded 26 in an FA Cup tie for Hyde United against Preston – an English club-record score to this date.

WALK THE WORLD ROUND

After retiring from the game, many players take up occupations that their playing careers never suggested. The most unusual one must, however, belong to the legendary Archie Goodall who spent some time touring both Europe and America with a strongman act that comprised of him walking around with a giant metal hoop.

WHAT A RECORD!

The Rams created one record in their first season of league football that they would hope never to break. They went on an eight-game losing streak from the end of September until early December. The sequence has twice been equalled, but thankfully never surpassed.

ISN'T HE LOVELY

Playing for the Rams has led to many awards and honours for individuals but so far John Harkes has been the only Derby County player to be voted into *People* magazine's annual '50 Most Beautiful People' list.

WHAT A CRACKER

By common consent, John Harkes scored one of the most spectacular goals ever seen at the Baseball Ground. Unfortunately, for the majority of the 17,050 crowd it was a time of despair not celebration as Harkes was part of the Sheffield Wednesday side that won that evening's FA Cup replay 2-1.

I OBJECT – AGAIN

The Rams appearance in the 1893 FA Cup competition could certainly be described as controversial. Derby lost away to Sheffield Wednesday and successfully protested that their opponents had fielded an ineligible player. They won the rematch, after which the Sheffield outfit complained that the Rams had fielded an ineligible player. The match was once again replayed, and this time Sheffield Wednesday won 4-2 with no complaints from Derby.

FROM DISTANT SHORES

John Harkes was not, by a long way, the first footballer to represent his country while in Derby colours. However, the USA cap he won against Switzerland in the 1994 World Cup finals made him the first current international outside the British Isles to play for the Rams.

ONE OVER THE EIGHT

If scoring four past Aston Villa hadn't been impressive enough for Sandy Higgins in 1888, he went one better the following season, netting all five in the 5-0 whitewash of Villa on December 28th.

FIVE ALIVE

When Sandy Higgins netted his five against Aston Villa, he achieved a feat that has only been equalled six times subsequently in club history. This means that you would have to watch the Rams for over 18 years before complaining that you were unlucky never to see a player hit five in one game.

TICKETS FOR SALE

Archie Goodall nearly missed the kick-off the first time that the Rams made an FA Cup final. Goodall had decided that there was money to be made on cup final tickets and ridiculously close to the start of the match was still outside trying to sell some of his surplus stock.

I'M OFF

John Harkes left Derby County, citing as one of his reasons for going the fact that he had been promised Premier League football. Ironic really as Harkes missed an open goal in the 1994 play-off final that would almost certainly have gained the club promotion had he converted it.

MISTER CONSISTENT

Archie Goodall may have justifiably had a reputation as a fiery individual who went his own way, but his consistency and availability for selection are beyond argument. He notched up 167 consecutive appearances in all competitions, and 151 in the league.

WHO'S IN GOAL?

John Goodall was renowned for his ability as a forward but, due to lack of available alternatives, was picked to keep goal on January 25th 1890 against Wolves. Derby lost, but Goodall couldn't have done too badly as he was only beaten twice in the 2-1 defeat.

ALWAYS THERE

For the first time in club history, the Rams had four ever-presents throughout the 1893/94 season. The players who never missed a game were John Allen, Archie Goodall, Johnny McMillan, and Jimmy Methven. This feat has so far only been equalled twice subsequently in club history.

FIRST FOR ENGLAND

Many Derby County players over the years have played for the England national side, but John Goodall could claim to be the first when he was selected to play against Wales on March 7th 1891.

JUST NOT CRICKET

Derby County once played in a Test match, although it was nothing to do with cricket. For the first few seasons that there were two divisions, there was no promotion or relegation as we know it. The bottom three teams in Division One met the top three in Division Two in a one-off match on neutral ground. The Rams beat Notts County 2-1 the only time they were involved. The game was at Walnut Street, Leicester, on April 27th 1895.

LONG, LONG, LONG

When Jimmy Methven made his debut for the Rams at Stoke on September 5th 1891 he could never have dreamt that he would be part of the club for the next 31 years. He played 511 times and then managed the club for 16 years.

BROTHER KNOWS BEST

It's not unusual for overseas players to have to do a bit of research about their new club ahead of completing a transfer. But when the Rams snapped up Australian international Mile Sterjovski from Turkish club Hacettepe in January 2008, the midfielder didn't need to look far. Rather than resort to the internet, all he needed to do was pick up the phone and call up his older brother Nick. For Nick, back in the late 1980s, had adopted Derby County as his team to follow in English football and filled in Mile with everything he needed to know. Nick eventually got over to Derby for the first time towards the end of the 2008/09 season and paid his first visit to Pride Park Stadium for a home defeat against Wolverhampton Wanderers – when, fittingly, Mile was on target with one of the Rams' goals in the 3-2 reverse. Derby's matchday programme caught up with the pair for a unique interview, during which Nick revealed that his love for the Rams stemmed from picking an underdog that was doing well – as Derby were at that time.

TWO HEADS BETTER THAN ONE?

Extra assistant referees for Champions League and Europa League games are yet to convince anyone that they are an ideal way to avoid controversial decisions. But such a radical change to the way matches are officiated is nothing new – way back in 1935, the Football League used a celebration game for the Jubilee of King George V to test running with two referees but no linesmen, as they have traditionally been known. The match in question was played at the Hawthorns when West Bromwich Albion hosted a Football League XI that included two Derby County stars, Jack Barker and Sammy Crooks. And there was a further connection as one of the men in the middle hailed from Derby – Dr Arthur Willoughby Barton, the head of physics at Repton School. The game itself proved entertaining enough as the Football League's team won it 9-6 but the experiment didn't last long. A month later, the Football League formally called a halt to the idea citing it as 'unworkable', and they returned to the tried and tested system of one referee and two other officials running the line.

MILE STERJOVSKI SIGNED FOR THE RAMS ON THE ADVICE GIVEN TO HIM BY HIS DERBY SUPPORTING BROTHER

BIGGEST FA CUP WIN

January 30th 1897 goes down in Derby County club history as the day they recorded their biggest ever score in the FA Cup. The visitors, then known as Barnsley St Peters, but now called Barnsley FC, were in town for an FA Cup tie that the Rams won 8-1. It remains their record victory in the competition.

RAMS OF TWO LEAGUES

For two seasons – 1893/94 and 1894/95 – the Rams competed in both the Football League Division One and the United Counties League. Formed around clubs in the East and West Midlands to give the sides extra games, the idea was quickly shelved as promotion and relegation became more important for teams.

ENGLAND'S DYNAMIC DUO

When Steve Bloomer made his international debut he must have felt at home straight away, partially because the game was played at the County Ground, Derby's home at the time, and also as his strike partner was John Goodall. The pair each netted twice as England beat Ireland 9-0.

OVER CONFIDENT?

The Rams must have been confident going into their first FA Cup final in 1898. They were matched up against local rivals Nottingham Forest who they had beaten by an impressive scoreline of 5-0 a mere five days earlier. Forest, however, treated the final as payback time, winning 3-1.

ALMOST THERE

Although they have only ever won the FA Cup once, Derby County were one of the most successful clubs during the early years of the competition. Starting from 1895 the Rams made the semi-finals in seven out of the next nine years. They reached the final itself on three of those occasions, but lost the lot.

CONSECUTIVE BEST

Only three times in their history have the Rams had four players feature in every league game of the campaign. The first was in 1893/94 when the season consisted of 30 games. The most recent was 1938/39 by which time the schedule had increased to 42 matches.

MOST GOALS IN A GAME

Amongst the many records that Steve Bloomer broke was that for most goals in a game. Bloomer scored no less than six against Sheffield Wednesday on January 21st 1899. Three others were put past the hapless Owls keeper to record a record-equalling 9-0 to the hosts.

TURN OF THE CENTURY

Steve Bloomer was so prolific that it only took him 151 games to score his first century of goals. Pleasingly for Derby fans, it came as part of a hat-trick against local rivals Nottingham Forest.

HAWTHORNS FIRST

As a West Midlander himself, Steve Bloomer would have enjoyed knowing that he scored the first goal at West Brom's ground, The Hawthorns. The date was September 3rd 1900, and his strike gave the Rams the lead. Albion struck back though and the match ended as a 1-1 draw.

SCHOOL COMES FIRST

Club versus country has long been an issue in football but professional against amateur is more unusual. It happened at Derby County with Reginald Hounsfield. Hounsfield was educated at Repton School. He always put playing for the Old Reptonians in the Arthur Dunn Cup ahead of Rams matches.

DEBUT HAT-TRICK

In spite of the Rams' long history, there is only one player to score a hat-trick on his Derby debut. The player in question is Ted Garry who was signed from Celtic. The match in question was a 4-0 win at home to Lincoln City. Ironically, it was the only hat-trick of Garry's Derby career.

WRONG PLACE WRONG TIME

As a goalscorer, Steve Bloomer was renowned for being in the right place at the right time. He found himself in quite the opposite situation after he finished playing, however. Bloomer went to Germany to take up a coaching job. He arrived a mere three weeks before the outbreak of World War I, and spent the entire conflict incarcerated in a civilian detention camp.

TOP TEN APPEARANCES – 8. SAMMY CROOKS

A north-easterner by birth, Sammy Crooks was one of 17 children and worked in the coal mines while playing locally until rheumatism forced him to abandon his career underground. In 1926 he signed for Durham City, who were then in the Third Division (North) and played there for just one season before Derby manager George Jobey spotted him and signed him up for £300. It's a fee that wouldn't even get you a season ticket these days but it proved to be money well spent as Sammy became one of the leading players in England and helped push Derby on to further successes. As an outside-forward or outside-right, he made 445 appearances for Derby over the next 20 seasons and scored 111 goals. Sammy made his debut on September 10th 1927 in a 2-1 win over Leicester City and that sparked one of the greatest careers in the club's history. Three years later he became an England international, playing in a 5-2 victory over Scotland for the first of his 26 international appearances. Sammy scored seven goals in those 26 games, including two in a 7-1 defeat of Spain, and he played his final match for England in 1936. Sammy helped Derby to finish runners-up in the Football League in 1930, and again in 1936, although by that time he could have left the club. In 1935 Arsenal tried to sign him and Tommy Cooper in exchange for the Gunners' Alex James, but the deal fell through as the Londoners also wanted a cash payment that Derby were not prepared to meet. It was a good job too as Sammy was a true inspiration for Derby and is one of the finest players ever to wear the club's colours. Unfortunately, his career was interrupted by World War II otherwise he would surely have added even more appearances and goals to his already superb record. During the war he guested for Nottingham Forest but was back in a Derby shirt for the 1946 FA Cup campaign when he scored in every round, until he was cruelly ruled out for the final – which the Rams won for the first and so far only time – by a knee injury. Sammy later moved into management and took charge locally at Gresley Rovers, Burton Albion and Heanor Town, and died in Belper in 1981. The club's Young Player of the Year award is now named the Sammy Crooks Trophy in his honour.

FIRST FOR WALES

Charlie Morris had already been capped by Wales before signing for Derby County, but his selection to play against Scotland at Wrexham made him the first Ram to represent the Principality.

BLOOMER BEATS DARLEY DALE

It was clear that Steve Bloomer had an eye for goal from the very beginning. On his first appearance in a Derby shirt he put four past Darley Dale. Ironically, it took him four games from his league debut to score his first competitive goal.

BAD LIGHT STOPS PLAY

In the days before floodlights, the Rams were denied victory over local rivals Chesterfield seven minutes from the end of extra-time because of bad light. They were 2-1 up at the time. The FA ruled that as a minimum of 90 minutes had already been played the rematch would be on a neutral ground. Derby duly won 4-0.

YOU WANT ME TO DO WHAT?

Arthur Latham must have thought his playing days were over when the full-back hung up his boots in 1890. He travelled with the team to Blackburn in his capacity as trainer but was pressed into service as an emergency goalkeeper when Tom Harrison, the regular custodian, missed the train. The Rams lost 3-1.

WELCOME VISITOR

Herbert Smith was on a social visit to Derbyshire when he was invited to turn out for the Rams. He made just the one appearance for Derby having won both full and amateur caps for England in his time. He went on to win gold for Great Britain in the 1908 London Olympics football competition.

STAR SALE

Rams fans were in shock in March 1906 as the unthinkable happened. Short of finance, Derby County took the drastic step of selling their star man Steve Bloomer to Middlesbrough. The club received £750 plus full-back Emor Ratcliffe. The sale proved to be a disastrous one as the Rams were relegated at the end of the following season.

SIXTEEN INTO THIRTY

As if to prove the wisdom of keeping a settled side, 1895/96 was the Rams' best season to that date. They played 30 games and finished third using only 16 different players; John Robinson, Jimmy Methven, Joseph Leiper, Jack Cox, Archie Goodall, George Kinsey, John Goodall, Steve Bloomer, John Miller, John McMillan, Hugh McQueen, Jonathon Staley, Philip Bloomer, James Stevenson, Percy Francis, and John Paul.

FAST TRACK

When Horace Barnes made his debut for Derby County reserves he could not have anticipated how quickly he would be promoted to the senior ranks. He played just the one game for the second string before being called into first-team action. He compounded matters by then scoring against Blackpool on his first-team debut.

INCREDIBLE SEQUENCE

Steve Bloomer ended the 1893/94 campaign as the Rams' leading scorer in the league. It was the start of a remarkable run that saw him keep the accolade for 13 seasons.

A TEST FOR FOOTBALLERS

Over the years four Derby County footballers have been chosen to play Test cricket for their country. The quartet is; William Chatterton, William Storer, Frank Sugg, and Arnold Warren.

FIRST BASEBALL GROUND GAME

March 19th 1892 marks the first occasion that the Rams played a home match at the Baseball Ground. There was a clash of interests at the Racecourse Ground. The football club realised that they would have to play second fiddle to the so-called sport of kings. Initially only playing one game at their temporary accommodation, the event set in motion what would prove to be 102 years of history at their soon-to-be-new permanent home.

200 AND STILL GOING

November 30th 1901 was a very special day for the prolific Steve Bloomer. The striker scored twice in the 3-1 victory over Everton. His second took his tally to 200 goals in 279 appearances. The other goal came courtesy of Arnold Warren.

SCORING KEEPER

When goalkeeper Ernald Scattergood scored from the penalty spot away to Manchester City on April 13th 1913, little did he realise that he would go down as the only goalkeeper in Derby history to score a competitive goal in a match. Although keepers have subsequently scored in penalty shoot-outs, Scattergood's three career goals make him unique.

FIRST TO THIRTY

With his goal in the 2-0 victory away to Preston on April 19th 1897, Steve Bloomer became the first Derby player to pass the 30 goals in a season mark. His total in league and FA Cup that season was 31.

RIGHT AT THE DEATH

Over the years, the Rams have made a habit of leaving things until the last possible moment. The club only cemented their promotion as champions back to Division One on the final day of the 1911/12 season. They took the title thanks to a better goal average than closest rivals Chelsea.

BEST START

The start of the 1905/06 season has, so far, proved to be the best in club history. The Rams won all of their first five games. They could not keep up such a blistering pace, however, and ended the season in 15th place.

FIRST TO 200

Archie Goodall was the first player in club history to register 200 appearances. The landmark was reached in a 2-0 away defeat at Liverpool on September 12th 1896. When Goodall finally left the Rams at the end of the 1902/03 season he had achieved a total of 423 appearances for the club, a total that has only been bettered on eight subsequent occasions.

GOOD TO BE BACK

He may have been 35 when he returned to Derby, but Steve Bloomer had an instant effect on Rams fans. Some 12,000 turned out to see his comeback game – 6,000 more than had witnessed the previous home fixture.

THE LAST TIME

When Steve Bloomer scored a brace in the 5-3 defeat at home to Sheffield United on September 6th 1913, no-one in the crowd realised that they would be Bloomer's last goals for the club. He played sporadically throughout the rest of the campaign, without finding the back of the net. He ended with a career total of 332 goals in 525 games. It was a grand total that is never likely to be beaten.

SHARP JOURNALIST

Ivan Sharpe was not only a regular for the Rams for two seasons between 1910 and 1912, but a journalist as well. On his CV he could include being editor of *Athletic News* and an Olympic gold medal winner with the Great Britain football team at the Stockholm Olympics.

LONG SERVANTS

Despite having a spell away from the club to play for Middlesbrough, Steve Bloomer's career record of 525 appearances has only been beaten by three players so far. The trio of long servers to achieve the feat are Ron Webster, Roy McFarland, and Kevin Hector. Bloomer was, of course, the only member of the quartet to reach his target before the outbreak of World War I. The other three all played during the greatest period of success for the Rams and each won two championship medals.

CUP FINAL TRIO

Three players took part in all three of Derby County's FA Cup final defeats at the turn of the 20th century. They were John Boag, Jack Fryer, and Jimmy Methven. It is rumoured that film footage actually exists of their 1899 defeat against Sheffield United that was played at Crystal Palace, although no-one has been able to trace its whereabouts or even if it is still in a watchable condition.

FIRST FOR IRELAND

The first Derby County player to be picked to play for Ireland was Archie Goodall who made his debut in Belfast, against Wales, on March 4th 1899.

TEN GREAT HOME MATCHES – DERBY 4 FOREST 1

The 1979/80 season was a disaster for the Rams from beginning to end. Only five wins and two draws out of the first 15 league games – and relegation. One of the high points of the last 35 years occurred, though, when local rivals Nottingham Forest were the visitors to the Baseball Ground. Forest were at the peak of their powers and with Peter Shilton, arguably the best keeper in the world at the time, between the sticks very few neutrals gave Derby a chance. Forest took the game to the hosts from the off but rarely troubled David McKellar in the home goal. Garry Birtles wasted a good chance by shooting wide, but with 13 minutes on the clock the unthinkable happened; the infallible Peter Shilton made a hash of dealing with a Steve Buckley cross and Gerry Daly was in the right position to open the scoring. The goal unsettled the double European Cup winners who suffered a nightmare five minutes that lost them the game. A flowing move involving five different outfield players ended with David Langan firing in a cross from the right that Shilton could only palm to John Duncan who headed home. With the Forest defence becoming increasingly rattled, Frank Gray set up the next Derby goal by messing up a back pass which Steve Emery snapped up and fired past the hapless Shilton for 3-0 with only 17 minutes gone. There was no further scoring ahead of the half-time interval. Unsurprisingly, Brian Clough used the break to galvanise his troops and Derby nerves started to jangle a little when John Robertson pulled a goal back after Daly had fouled Gary Mills in the area. There was a desire not to let things slip – which had been missing in previous Rams performances – and the hosts began to recover their composure. Duncan nearly increased the lead after the pass of the game from Jonathon Clark. With 77 minutes gone Duncan made the result safe. David Needham, who had been conceding free kicks throughout the match, committed a foul that allowed free-kick specialist Buckley to provide an opportunity for Duncan to head his second of the game. The game provided a timely lift for the crowd. Unfortunately, the win did nothing to improve their league position and another 13 games would pass before the home side tasted victory again – and by then it was too late.

FIRST PAST BLOOMER

It fell to Alf Bentley to break the 24 league-goal mark that Steve Bloomer had achieved on three separate occasions. Bentley netted 27 in the league and one in the cup in 1908/09.

TOMMY BENFIELD

Tommy Benfield was not the only footballer to have his career destroyed by World War I, but his story was one of the most poignant. He was an ever-present in his one season with the Rams, scoring 15 goals. He made the rank of sergeant in the Leicestershire Regiment, and died in action on November 10th 1918, just one day before peace was declared.

FROM ONCE TO GREATNESS

Stuart McMillan is one of a small group who both played for, and managed, the Rams. His success as a manager is there for all to see – he was in charge of the only Derby County side to win the FA Cup. His playing career for the club is considerably more modest, however. He played just once in a 1-1 draw at home to Glossop on January 2nd 1915.

WAY TOO FEW

If goals are the lifeblood of the game, it is unsurprising that the Rams found themselves in a critical condition at the end of the 1920/21 season. Their total of 32 was a club-record low that lasted into the 21st century. It goes without saying that the campaign ended in relegation.

LOWEST GOAL DISASTER

Derby's disastrous campaign in the Premier League in the 2007/08 season was record-breaking for many reasons. For one, they broke their lowest number of goals scored by some considerable distance as they netted just 20 all campaign.

NO GOALS TODAY

Many Derby fans felt that a proven striker would have made the club's return to the top flight in 2007/08 easier. They were almost certainly right as the top four goalscorers on the Premier League list that term each individually managed to hit the back of the net more times than the entire Derby team. The team managed 20 goals!

CARRYING ON AS BEFORE

Despite not returning to the club until six games into the campaign, Steve Bloomer still managed to end the 1910/11 season as leading scorer, as he had done every year until he left for Middlesbrough.

UNLIKELY RETURN

At the age of 40, Harry Maskrey had every right to believe that his professional career was over. Despite only playing for British Cellulose in the Works League, the Rams called on him in a goalkeeping crisis. In 1920, he played five times in all. The Rams drew the first of them but then lost the remaining four.

WORST EVER DEFENSIVE RECORD

In the disastrous Premier League campaign of 2007/08, not only was the forward line weak, but the defence regularly got turned over by potent opposing strike forces. Derby's end-of-season goal difference was minus 69. The gap between the Rams and champions Manchester United in goal difference was a whopping 127.

NOWHERE NEAR

The Rams were so far out of their depth in the 2007/08 season that they ended up a staggering 25 points shy of safety, and 24 points adrift of Birmingham City, the club immediately above them. Unsurprisingly, they suffered the earliest relegation in Premier League history.

TOO LONG

Paul Jewell took charge of the Rams in time for their defeat away to Sunderland on December 1st 2007. It took until September 13th 2008 to register his first league victory as Derby boss, a 2-1 win at home to Sheffield United, in a sequence that took in 30 matches. This is by some considerable distance the longest stretch from commencing the job to winning a game.

FALSE DAWN

After a six-goal mauling at the hands of Liverpool at Anfield, the Rams bounced back with a 1-0 win at home to Newcastle United in front of the television cameras on September 17th 2007. Any supporters who thought a corner had been turned were proved sadly wrong. This was the only Premier League victory of the Rams' entire campaign.

BLANK CZECHS

During his time as owner of Derby County, Robert Maxwell thought he had pulled off a huge coup by providing Derby with two international players from Czechoslovakia – the land of his birth. The pair, who were named Ivo Knoflicek and Lubos Kubic, became familiar faces around the training ground and showed that they had undoubted skill. Rams fans never got to see them play as Fifa would not sanction the signings.

THEY FAILED

Despite the calamitous nature of the Rams' 2007/08 Premier League campaign, not every opponent turned them over. Neither Fulham nor Newcastle tasted victory. Fulham managed a draw both home and away, while Newcastle only avoided defeat both home and away thanks to a late Mark Viduka equaliser at St James' Park.

NO SIX APPEAL

To concede six goals in a single match is disappointing to say the least. The Rams managed it four times in the disastrous 2007/08 Premier League campaign. They also let in five on two occasions and four on four (including a home defeat by Championship outfit Preston in the FA Cup).

NO GOALS

The Rams failed to score in an incredible 22 matches out of 38 during their worst-ever top-flight season in 2007/08. In the same campaign they also only registered three clean sheets.

36 IN 38

Some 36 different players appeared for the Rams in their 2007/08 Premier League campaign. Four players made six starts between them while Paris Simmons registered his sole Derby County appearance as a late substitute in the final match of the season at home to Reading.

34-YEAR-OLD DEBUTANT

Derby County found themselves represented in the first international match after the end of World War I. The honour fell to Jimmy Bagshaw who won his one and only cap at the age of 34 in Belfast. Bagshaw featured for England in a 1-1 draw against Ireland in 1919.

MISSING THE WHITE HORSE

The introduction of Cecil Potter as the Rams' manager brought an instant change in fortune as the club were once again within a whisker of the FA Cup final in the 1922/23 season. Their charge for glory came to an end with a 5-2 defeat by West Ham United in the semi-final played at Stamford Bridge. The final in question was the first to be played at Wembley, and the loss denied Derby a place in football legend.

POOLS TO RAMS

Brian Clough is renowned for moving from Hartlepools to take over managing the Rams. It is also widely known that he did everything from painting the ground to running the first team in his time at the Victoria Ground. He wasn't, however, the first. Cecil Potter had been secretary, player, and manager at Hartlepools before taking up the Derby County hot seat way back in 1922.

MERRY CHRISTMAS CRYSTAL PALACE

Jimmy Moore ensured that it was a miserable Christmas for all connected with Crystal Palace by scoring five goals in a 6-0 drubbing of the Londoners on December 25th 1922. Moore's reward was his one and only cap at the age of 34 for England against Sweden in Stockholm.

BADLY MISTAKEN

A 3-2 win at the Baseball Ground for Bristol City must have given them confidence that when the return match was played a week later they would be able to widen the margin because of home advantage. The Robins were certainly right in thinking the margin would be wider, but wrong in assuming things would fall their way. The Rams, however, returned home with an 8-0 victory – Derby's biggest away win.

STORER OF GOALS

Harry Storer was one of that small and select band who both played for and managed the Rams. His greatest season as a Derby County player was 1923/24 when he was leading scorer with 27 goals in all competitions. His tally was boosted by hitting four in a game on two separate occasions, against Bristol City away, and Nelson at home.

TOP TEN APPEARANCES – 7. GEOFF BARROWCLIFFE

Geoff Barrowcliffe was a fine example of a player being spotted locally while working in an industry, and going on to enjoy an excellent career as a professional footballer. He was born in Ilkeston in October 1931 and began as a non-league player with his local club before being spotted and snapped up by the Rams in October 1950. The club showed their faith in him a year later when giving him a debut against Stoke City. They were paid off handsomely over the next 16 years with service that was as loyal and consistent as it was packed with quality on the football field. Geoff, equally at home both as a left-back or right-back, made 503 appearances for Derby County and played in the First Division, Second Division, and Third Division (North) as the Rams suffered two relegations before winning promotion in 1957. He would often appear as a centre forward too, if required, and never looked out of place wherever he lined up on the pitch because of his natural ability and that knack of simply enjoying playing the game. Geoff missed just one game of the 1957 promotion-winning campaign and as well as his consistency in performance, he was also clinical in front of goal with 37 strikes during his time as a player, many from the penalty spot. But, as well as his performances on the field, Geoff was known as a gentleman off it, respected by players, managers, coaching staff and supporters alike for his manners and politeness. He was originally signed by Stuart McMillan and went on to serve under Jack Barker, Harry Storer and Tim Ward, all of whom recognised how important a player he was to the team. After finishing his career with Derby, Geoff dropped into the non-league game to play for Boston United from 1966 for a year, and then later turned out for Heanor Town, Moor Green Colliery, Kimberley Town and Long Eaton United, before managing Kimberley and Radford. And, he also continued to play regularly in a Derby shirt into his 60s, turning out in various fundraising matches. Geoff sadly died in October 2009 at the age of 77, just a few weeks before he would have turned 78, and glowing tributes were paid to the man who gave such sterling service to the Rams. A minute's silence was held in his memory ahead of a first-team match at Pride Park Stadium, while another was held two days later before an already-scheduled friendly encounter between Derby and Ilkeston – two of his teams.

MARGIN OF FAILURE

Success or failure can be separated by the narrowest margins, but you would struggle to have a much smaller margin than 0.015 of a goal. Incredibly, though, Derby failed to gain promotion back to the top flight by such an amount in the days of goal average (dividing the number of goals scored by the number conceded). Just one more goal for the Rams would have been enough to tip the balance in their favour.

BACK OF A LORRY

When George Jobey signed the legendary Sammy Crooks for Derby he could honestly say that he got the player off the back of a lorry. Crooks played for Third Division side Durham City, and the Rams boss signed him at the end of his coal delivery round.

FROM TENANT TO LANDLORD

After 29 years as tenants, Derby County became owners of the Baseball Ground in July 1924. The price they had to pay the then owner was just £10,000.

NO MORE GUESSING

The knowledge of just how much support the Rams had became reality in 1926. Prior to the start of that season attendances had been no more than estimates. The first time the actual crowd size was shown at the Baseball Ground was August 31st 1925 when the visit of Clapton Orient attracted 13,403. Of course, for many years there was a belief that the figures were still not as accurate as they might be.

STEPHENSON'S ROCKETS

George Stephenson joined the elite group of Rams players to net four or more goals in a match when his team beat Grimsby Town 5-4 on December 14th 1929.

NEVER THE SAME

The 1898/99 season was average in many ways. The Rams finished halfway up the table and the campaign before saw a defeat to Nottingham Forest in the FA Cup final. One way this particular season did differ is that for the first time since the formation of the Football League in 1888, Derby did not manage a single ever-present throughout all the league fixtures.

AS GOOD AS A B C

Two years after purchasing the Baseball Ground from Sir Francis Ley, Derby County had a main stand to be proud of. Built along the Shaftesbury Crescent side of the ground, the A, B, and C stands – as they became known – were opened in September 1926, and remained a feature of the stadium right until the operation was moved to Pride Park some 70 years later.

GREAT MOVE

When Jack Bowers moved from playing Midland League football for Scunthorpe and Lindsey United to Division One Derby County, it proved a spectacular success. An ever-present from the tenth game of the 1930/31 season onwards, he hit 37 league goals in the season including four in a game three times. That total has subsequently been equalled but never bettered.

TOP TOTAL

When George Stephenson scored the lone Rams goal in the 2-1 defeat away to Birmingham on May 5th 1928 he ensured that the 'goals for' total for that season read 96. It is a top-division total that has been equalled subsequently, but never beaten.

FIRST IN THE CUP

When Harry Bedford put four past Bradford City on January 8th 1927 he was not the first Derby player to have scored that many in a single match. He was, though, the first of only two to date to score that many in an FA Cup tie.

BEST YET

A 4-2 win against Arsenal on October 11th 1930 set a club record of 23 consecutive games without defeat. It is a run that has been equalled but not yet beaten.

CUP-WINNING CAPTAIN

Jack Nicholas was not the only player to feature for the Rams on both sides of World War II. He only played three league games after the war, but he was a key part of Derby's greatest-ever day. He was captain the day that Derby won the FA Cup for the first, and so far only, time.

HAT-TRICK ZERO AND HERO

The FA Cup third-round tie at home to lowly Bristol Rovers on January 3rd 2002 was a disappointment for Rams fans as once again their team underperformed against a side they were expected to beat. Nathan Ellington did the damage with a hat-trick. When Ellington moved to Pride Park for the 2008/09 campaign he scored three against Lincoln City in the League Cup, making him that rarest of players who has scored hat-tricks both for and against the Rams.

FIRST RECORD CROWD

The construction of a main stand at Derby allowed for an increase in capacity, and with official attendances, rather than estimates, only recently introduced, December 27th 1926 saw a then record 30,557 turn out to see the Rams beat Bolton Wanderers 2-0.

STEPHENSON AND STEPHENSON

George and Bob Stephenson are another father and son combination to play for the Rams. George netted 56 goals in 120 games. His son only played 14 times, scoring one goal in the process, but went on to enjoy a decent career as a county cricketer.

NEVER AGAIN

At the time of writing, the Rams have met 99 different clubs in league action throughout their history. Only two of them have been in opposition for one solitary season. They are Colchester United and Nelson. Colchester have also been FA Cup opponents more than once.

EFFORTS IN VAIN

You would have thought that Jack Bowers would have been delighted to add his name to the few who have scored in six consecutive games for the Rams. He hit the back of the net 15 times during the run but still managed to end up on the losing side in three of the games.

NOW THAT'S RELIABLE!

Jack Nicholas was as reliable as it is possible to be as a player. Starting during the 1931/32 season and finishing at the end of the 1938/39 campaign he missed only three games out of a possible 331 Football League matches.

FATHER AND SON

Gary Bowyer never actually played football for the Rams but was, for a spell, a successful youth-team coach for Derby. His father Ian had played for local rivals Nottingham Forest. Bowyer senior was manager at Hereford United where son Gary briefly played. A match away to Scunthorpe United in 1990 made them the last father and son pairing to play a senior competitive fixture in the same team.

FIRST SCOTTISH INTERNATIONAL

It was not until 1932 that Derby County presented the Scotland national side with their first player. That honour fell to Dally Duncan who was chosen to play against Wales.

RAMS' ROKER RECORD

When Sunderland were drawn away to Derby in the 1933 FA Cup the tie attracted a record-breaking 34,218 crowd. The game was drawn and the replay attracted a staggering 75,118 to Roker Park. It is a Sunderland record that is unlikely to ever be beaten.

ACCEPT NO SUBSTITUTE

Colin Boulton was not the only player to feature in both the league championship wins in the 1970s. He was, though, so consistent and injury free that he was an ever-present throughout both seasons. Almost as impressive was his team-mate Kevin Hector who, despite the physical abuse suffered by all strikers, missed only four out of a possible 84 games during the two campaigns.

MOST FREQUENT OPPONENT

The honour of facing the Rams the most number of times in league action falls to Wolverhampton Wanderers. Derby County have lined up against the Wolves – as at the end of 2010/11 – on 132 occasions.

PLAYER 1,000

When Theo Robinson signed on loan from Millwall in time to be named in the Rams squad to play a home game against Hull City on February 22nd 2011, he could not have realised that his name would go down forever in Derby County history. His 64th-minute introduction into the game made him the 1,000th player to make a senior competitive appearance.

RECORD LEAGUE AGGREGATE

The Rams registered their record aggregate league score on September 6th 1890. The visitors were Blackburn Rovers, and the match ended 8-5 in favour of the hosts, an aggregate total of 13 that has yet to be beaten.

HIGHEST SCORER IN SEASON

Amongst his many achievements, Jack Bowers was Division One's leading scorer in the 1932/33 season. His total in all competitions was 43, which included eight FA Cup goals. It remains a Rams record today.

HEANOR OLD BOYS

The 0-0 draw played out at the Walkers Stadium on October 17th 2009 was, in many ways, a dull and uninteresting affair. The opposing managers Nigel Clough and Nigel Pearson had a unique bond between them, however. Both had started their playing careers at lowly Heanor Town. Surely the first – and up to that point only – time that the Derbyshire club had contributed to a Championship match in such a manner.

BEST SCORING RUN

Jack Bowers holds the record for the best individual scoring run in Derby County history. He found the back of the net in seven consecutive games. It started on January 3rd and ended on February 14th 1931. It wasn't just a goal a game he managed. He actually netted 17 in total.

BLAME THE REF

A dubious record of some kind was set on February 3rd 1900. The referee disallowed no less than five goals by the Rams in a match away at Aston Villa. As a result the visitors ended up on the wrong end of a 3-2 scoreline.

ORMONDROYD ROCKS

Ian Ormondroyd, as far as anyone knows, is the only Derby County footballer, past or present, to have a rock band named in his honour. The band from Sheffield named themselves after the lanky striker, and released an album titled Hit & Hope (presumably also as a reference to the Bradford City, Leicester City, and Derby front man). Unlike Ormondroyd himself, the band seemed to enjoy a very short career.

THE LINESMAN STRIKES TWICE

Every football fan knows about the controversial Geoff Hurst goal in the 1966 World Cup final, and the part played by a linesman whose name was Tofik Bakhramov. Rams fans had a chance to see Bakhramov in action nine years later. He officiated at a European Cup tie at the Baseball Ground. On this occasion he helped the English side by disallowing a Madrid goal.

FIRST PRIDE PARK GOAL

Stefano Eranio holds the honour of scoring the first goal at Pride Park in a competitive match. His goal came from the penalty spot and was the decisive moment in a 1-0 victory over Barnsley on August 30th 1997.

RAMS STRIKE OIL

Derby County sold ground rights to the Texaco Oil Company for advertising in 1971. The two-year deal saw the Texaco logo, and advertising, plastered all over the Baseball Ground and was the first major sponsorship deal by any club in the country.

JUMPERS FOR GOALPOSTS

Woolly jumpers and cardigans may not sound terribly exciting but those produced by local firm Cox Moore of Long Eaton led to a fascinating first as the Rams were the first club in the country to sell sponsorship of an individual game, with Cox Moore writing their name into football legend in 1972.

PAST HIS BEST

Dave Mackay was considered past his best when brought by Brian Clough to the Baseball Ground in 1968 but led the club to promotion as captain. Ironically for a player with a 19-year career, he was an ever-present only once in that time. It was, in fact, his last-ever full season at Derby County – the 1970/71 campaign.

WEMBLEY LORD'S DOUBLE

Colin Boulton has the distinction of playing at the spiritual homes of both cricket and football in this country. He represented the Rams in the 1975 FA Charity Shield at Wembley and also featured for Dunstall Cricket Club at Lord's.

NEARLY BUT NOT QUITE

Ashley Ward was desperately unlucky not to have a unique double to his name. The centre forward scored in the last competitive first-team fixture at the Baseball Ground – in the 3-1 defeat against Arsenal. He was also the first player to find the back of the net at Pride Park in an evening game, against Wimbledon. Unfortunately for Ward, the game was abandoned midway through the second half when the floodlights failed, thus wiping his strike from the record books.

RAMS HOST CUP FINAL

The Rams were chosen to host the first FA Cup final played away from London. The initial match between Blackburn Rovers and West Bromwich Albion had ended in a goalless draw. Rovers won the replay at the County Ground 2-0 in front of an impressive crowd of 15,000.

FIRST-EVER HOME WIN

It took the Rams six attempts to register their first-ever win in front of a home crowd. The 3-2 victory over Notts County was registered on December 22nd 1888, and came after a sequence of eight straight defeats at home and on the road.

BAKEWELL'S SLICE OF THE CAKE

George Bakewell may have only scored 12 goals in his six-year spell with the Rams but he earned his place in club history with the first of them as it was also the first-ever competitive Derby County goal. It came on the first day of the 1888/89 season on September 8th 1888 in the 6-3 away win against Bolton Wanderers.

THE FIRST SUB

Bobby Saxton's career record for the Rams shows that he started 94 league matches and came off the bench on two further occasions. The first of those two gives him a place in Derby County folklore as the first player in club history to appear from the bench. His 15th-minute appearance as a sub at home to Southampton on August 21st 1965 to replace the injured Geoff Barrowcliffe was a mere two minutes too late to make him the first-ever sub in England.

FIRST SCOTTISH SUB

When the Scottish FA decided to introduce the substitution rule that allowed a team to make one change during the game to replace a player who was injured, the honour of being the very first fell to a young player from St Mirren named Archie Gemmill.

FIRST HOME FRIENDLY

It seems incredible but Derby County had been in existence for over 80 years before what has been described by various sources as the first official home friendly match. The game on August 11th 1965 saw the Rams take on Sheffield United.

SHIRTS OFF THEIR BACKS

It is often suggested that a team is 'not themselves' on a given day. It happened quite literally to Derby County on April 12th 1969. They arrived at The Den, apparently unaware of a colour clash between their shirts and those of hosts Millwall. The south London outfit offered their red away shirts for the afternoon to solve the problem. The Rams won 1-0 and probably confused both home and visiting supporters at the same time.

GOT THE BLUES

In a typically perverse piece of thinking, the FA decided at one stage that it would be sensible to rule that if there were a colour clash between two sides in a match both would have to change strip. Visitors to the Baseball Ground on March 17th 1973 found themselves, therefore, watching a sixth-round tie with hosts Derby kitted out entirely in blue and visitors Leeds United dressed from head-to-toe in red.

THINGS LOOK BLACK FOR REF

Fred Graham did not exactly make himself popular with the Derby County kit men when he rejected both the white home and the blue away strips as being potential colour clashes for the Rams away game against Brighton & Hove Albion at Withdean Stadium on February 5th 2005. Mr Graham, who was referee for the match, did not make his decision until the team had arrived at the ground, and the Rams were forced to play in their numbered black training kit.

LONGEST BARREN RUN

Disastrous though the Rams' 2007/08 Premier League campaign may have been, they did not manage to overtake a miserable record that the club had set in 1920. Derby failed to net a single goal from the end of October until Christmas Day. The barren run comprised of eight games and 720 minutes of actual playing time.

THE VERY LATE TITLE WIN

Many people would argue that it could only happen to Derby – winning a championship title in the wrong season. To add games to a sparse fixture list the United Counties League was introduced briefly in the 1890s. A drawn final match against West Bromwich Albion to decide the winners meant a replay that could not be scheduled into the fixtures until the following campaign. By the time that there was space in the fixture list it was the 1894/95 season. The Rams won, and therefore became the first, and probably only, side to win a championship in the wrong season.

THE CUSTOMER IS ALWAYS RIGHT

Whether Phil Brown was actually dismissed as Rams boss due to supporter power is open to debate, even though he lost much backing from the fans after publicly criticising them live on radio. One fan, though, got his own back via the airwaves. After Derby lost an FA Cup tie at Colchester on January 29th 2006, one very disgruntled supporter weighed into a live post-match interview being held on the Colchester pitch and berated Brown long and hard despite the requests from journalists for it to stop. The fan got his wish as the manager was dismissed within 48 hours.

ALMOST NEVER ENDING STORY

When Division Two Derby County were drawn against Newcastle United from the top flight in the 1924 FA Cup, no-one could have anticipated how much the two teams would see of each other. Drawn at home, the Rams earned a 2-2 draw and a replay at St James' Park. The game ended with the same scoreline after extra-time and a second replay on neutral ground produced exactly the same outcome. The third replay returned to Newcastle, and this time the Division One outfit ran out 5-3 victors.

SIGNIFICANT FIRST

The Watney Cup may not have the magic of the FA Cup, or even the League Cup in its various guises, but it was the first significant piece of silverware won by Brian Clough's Rams. They beat Manchester United 4-1 to win it in 1970. It provided Derby with another interesting first as it was the first sponsored Football League competition. It ran for another three seasons with Colchester United winning in 1971, Bristol Rovers (1972) and Stoke City (1973).

FOREVER A RAM

When Tim Ward moved from Cheltenham Town for a sum of £100 little did he realise that his future would be connected, on and off, to that of Derby County for the next 30 years. He played 260 games for the club between 1937 and 1950. Appointed as manager of the club as replacement for Harry Storer, he was in charge from 1962 to 1967 and brought both Alan Durban and Kevin Hector to the club. He never truly left the Rams and could often be seen playing for the ex Derby County all-stars well into his 60s.

30 IN A SEASON

The Rams have only had their leading goalscorer reach, or pass, the 30-goal mark seven times in their entire history. The full roll of honour is as follows:

Steve Bloomer	31 goals	1896/97
Alf Bentley	32 goals	1908/09
Alf Bentley	30 goals	1909/10
Harry Bedford	30 goals	1929/30
Jack Bowers	39 goals	1930/31
Jack Bowers	43 goals	1932/33
Ray Straw	37 goals	1956/57

BIRTH OF THE OSSIE END

Many older supporters will remember the two-tier Osmaston End Stand at the Baseball Ground, or 'the Ossie End' as it was popularly known. You would need to be a fair age to have attended the opening though as it was completed for the start of the 1933/34 season.

TOP TEN APPEARANCES – 6. JIMMY METHVEN

Jimmy Methven spent over 30 years associated with Derby County in one capacity or another and racked up more than 1,000 games in various roles. Over 500 of them – 511 to be precise – came in his playing days, which were spent at the club from 1891 to 1906. Born in Fife, Jimmy had played north of the border in Edinburgh with Leith Athletic, Heart of Midlothian and St Bernard's before signing for the Rams at the end of the 1890/91 season. He was a member of the squad that included the Goodall brothers, Archie and John, as well as legendary goalscorer Steve Bloomer. Jimmy is one of three players to have appeared in the three unsuccessful FA Cup finals of 1898, 1899 and 1903 and is a true legend of Derby County's early days due to his great service as a player, a robust right-back who was a member of the squad that adhered to the 'work hard, play hard' principle. Jimmy was such a star of the game during his playing days that he was described by one sporting journalist of the time as 'one of the wonders of the football world'. He chose to play his last game for the Rams on October 6th 1906 at home to Middlesbrough, who included Bloomer in their squad, the striker having been sold to Boro much to the anger of the Derby faithful. Derby won 1-0, and Jimmy took to the field wearing a Scottish representative cap, and then kept it on during the game. Though he could somewhat do as he chose having been appointed manager at the start of the season, immediately following the departure of Harry Newbould. Derby were relegated in that first season and showed no real signs of a return to the top flight over the next four years until Jimmy pulled off a master-stroke by convincing Bloomer to re-sign for the club. In 1911/12 they went back up as champions, only to be relegated again two years later, then bounce straight back again for a second promotion under Jimmy. World War I held Derby's progress up but Jimmy remained in charge when football resumed, and he left in June 1922 having been in charge for 498 games. His son, also called Jimmy, played one game for the club in 1913/14 while Jimmy senior remained in Derby until his death aged 84 in 1953. His grave is at a cemetery near Sunnyhill, on Stenson Road. As if finding a new permanent base to play football once it became apparent that groundsharing at the County Ground was problematic, the Rams also had to contend with a group of gypsies encamped on the land surrounding the Baseball Ground pitch. The camp was removed, but at some considerable cost to the fortunes of the football club as the departing gypsies left a curse that Derby County would achieve no real success until they had been appeased.

RECORD CROWD'S DELIGHT

The largest attendance at the Baseball Ground prior to the outbreak of World War II was 37,830. The match was an FA Cup fourth-round tie against local rivals Nottingham Forest. The majority of the crowd were delighted to witness a 2-0 win by the home side.

A SEASON TO REMEMBER

It was a sign of how strong the club was from top to bottom in the 1935/36 campaign when the Rams reserves won the Central League title for the first time in their history while the senior side finished in second place in Division One. They finished eight points shy of the 56 total gained by winners Sunderland.

RAMS PUB BAN

Peter Doherty was one of the stars for the Rams during and immediately after World War II, but left the club because of a dispute with the Derby County board over alcohol. Doherty wanted to take over the running of the Arboretum Hotel but the directors refused him permission to do so. As a result Doherty left the club and went to play for Huddersfield Town.

CHRISTMAS BLUES

There is no doubt that goalkeepers like to celebrate their debuts with clean sheets. The unfortunate Ken Scattergood was probably pleased that the tally did not reach double figures. Son of Ernald Scattergood, a one-time Rams and England keeper, Ken let in seven on his first appearance against Everton away on Christmas Day 1936. He kept his place for the Boxing Day home tie against West Bromwich Albion and played his part in a 1-0 win.

LOCAL HERO

At the end of Alf Bentley's Derby career he had netted 112 goals in 168 games. This gave him an average that put him ahead of the great Steve Bloomer. Unlike Bloomer, though, Bentley was born locally. His career both started and ended at the place of his birth – Alfreton. In between playing for the Rams and Alfreton Town he featured for Bolton Wanderers and West Bromwich Albion.

WORST HOME DEFEAT

January 29th 1938 was a miserable day for Rams fans everywhere as for the first time in their history the team was beaten by a score of 7-1 at home by Manchester City. It remains a record scoreline that has been equalled twice, but thankfully never surpassed, even during the disastrous season of 2007/08.

THE CAPTAIN AND THE GYPSY

It may have been merely that the best team won the 1946 FA Cup final, but there are those who will argue that the defining factor was a visit by Rams captain Jack Nicholas to a group of gypsies. He crossed their palms with silver and persuaded them to lift a curse that had supposedly been in place since the end of the 19th century.

FIRST WEMBLEY DEFEAT

In many respects Arthur Cox was one of the most successful managers in Derby County history. The only real stain on his record was that he was the first Rams manager to lose at Wembley. Stuart McMillan led the team to FA Cup glory in 1946, while Dave Mackay was at the helm for the Charity Shield victory in 1975. Defeat against US Cremonese in the final of the Anglo-Italian Cup by a score of 3-1 on March 27th 1993 was the first time the club had tasted defeat at the national stadium.

FOUR FOR ALL

The 1938/39 season ended with four players ever-present throughout the entire campaign. This had happened twice before in the club's history, but in the days of a 30-game season. This quartet had each played 42 league games. They were Ronnie Dix, Dally Duncan, Ralph Hann and Jack Nicholas.

BREAKING UP IS EASY

It is a commonly stated footballing belief that you should never change a winning side, but that is precisely what happened to the Rams after their one and only FA Cup final win. Four of the players from that historic victory had departed before the start of the next campaign and the winning side, therefore, never actually played a single post-war league match together.

1946 FA CUP RUN

January 5th............	Luton Town (a)...	.6-0 win
January 9th............	Luton Town (h)	.3-0 win
January 26th.........	West Bromwich Albion (h).........................	.1-0 win
January 30th.........	West Bromwich Albion (a)	.3-1 win
February 9th	Brighton & Hove Albion (a)	.4-1 win
February 13th	Brighton & Hove Albion (h).......................	.6-0 win
March 2nd............	Aston Villa (a)	.4-3 win
March 9th..............	Aston Villa (h)...	.1-1 draw
March 23rd...........	Birmingham City (neutral ground)	.1-1 draw
March 27th...........	Birmingham City (neutral ground)	.4-0 win
April 27th	Charlton Athletic (Wembley)......................	.4-1 win

STEELY PERFORMANCE

Billy Steel was one Ram who almost took on the world and won. Well, if not the world, Europe at least. Steel scored for Great Britain in a 6-1 win over a Rest of Europe team in May 1947 in a match arranged to celebrate the return of United Kingdom countries to Fifa. The match was watched by 134,000.

RECORD-BREAKING SEMI

The Rams may have fallen short of yet another FA Cup semi-final appearance when they lost 2-1 at Portsmouth on February 26th 1949, but they once again wrote their way into the record books by attracting a crowd of 51, 385 to Fratton Park – a record that has yet to be broken.

WHAT A SIGNING

George Jobey knew that he had obtained a quality player in Dai Astley when he brought him from Aston Villa, but even the Rams boss would have been amazed how successful the striker would be. He played 30 matches in his first season (1936/37) and scored 29 times.

POPULAR INMATE

Steve Bloomer proved to be so popular with his fellow inmates at the German civilian detention centre in Ruhleben that when he left in March 1918 they held a farewell football match in his honour. Bloomer had been incarcerated in Ruhleben for the entirety of World War I up to that point.

LONGEST CUP RUN

In order to reach the 1946 FA Cup final the Rams had to play ten games. The FA had decided that for the first competition after the war all matches up to the semi-final would be played on a home and away basis with aggregate scores deciding the winner of each round. The tenth game was a semi-final replay after the first game was drawn.

THE BIGGEST PRIZE

When the Rams made it to the Championship play-off final on May 28th 2007 it was considered the most valuable prize in football. The combination of increased revenue through the gates and via television appearances, along with parachute payments for two seasons in the event of relegation, made victory worth approximately £60m.

ONLY A GAME?

The phrase 'it's only a game' may well have echoed round the thoughts of those Derby fans that had travelled down to Millwall to watch the second leg of the 1993/94 play-off semi-final. Already 2-0 up from the home game, the match at the New Den took place in an increasingly hostile atmosphere. After the game, which the Rams won 3-1, sections of the Millwall crowd got so incensed that riot police on horseback were called out into the streets and a marked car belonging to the Radio Derby commentary team was turned over in the official club car park.

FASTEST GOAL EVER!

On April 25 1964, Jim Fryatt scored a goal for Bradford Park Avenue against Tranmere Rovers that was timed at four seconds from kick-off by the match referee. It still retains a place in the record books as the fastest-ever league goal. It gets a mention here as soon-to-be Derby legend Kevin Hector was involved in the build-up by playing the ball through to Fryatt.

LAST TO PLAY BOTH

Alan Ramage is the last cricketer/footballer to play both sports at senior level. The centre-half was signed from Middlesbrough in 1980 but managed only 38 games for the Rams before succumbing to injury. He played cricket for Yorkshire until 1983.

A HOSTILE NIGHT AT THE NEW DEN FOR THE 1994 PLAYOFF SEMI-FINAL

100 FOR NOW

When young goalkeeper James Seven came off the bench to replace the injured Stephen Bywater during the home defeat to Hull City on February 22nd 2011, he became player number 100 to make only one senior competitive appearance for the Rams. Ironically, if he had been the second substitute of the night he, rather than Millwall loanee Theo Robinson, would have become the 1,000th player to feature for Derby County too.

YOUR GO WILSON

If you are looking for a long career as a footballer at Derby County it is best not to have the surname Wilson. In the list of players to only make one appearance there are only four names duplicated. Smith unsurprisingly features more than once, while two Lanes and two Selveys are also included. There are, though, three different Wilsons out of a grand total of 1,000 players.

THE BISHOP AND THE FOOTBALL

It is difficult to judge how good a footballer the Reverend Llewellyn Henry Gwynne was as he only featured for the Rams once. He clearly felt a higher calling as he became a missionary in East Africa before becoming Bishop of Khartoum. At the end of World War I he became Bishop of Egypt and Sudan.

HIS NAME WAS WHAT?

The following is a list of some of the more interestingly named individuals to feature for the Rams over the years; Shirley Wray Abbott, Hervey Bayliss, Enos Bromage, Noah Burton, Horatio Stratton Carter, Septimus Randolph Galloway, Verdun Aubrey Jones, Errington Ridley Liddell Keen, Moses Lane, Haydn Morley, Gresham Parnell, Reuben Pitman, Algernon Pynegar, Emor Ratcliffe, Valentine Norman Rowe, Reginald Alphonsus Ryan, Earnald Oak Scattergood, Elijah Solomon Tremelling, Levi George Wright.

TWO AT ONCE

Since the creation of the England international side, there have been 39 players capped for their country while on Derby's books, a list which includes Benjamin Spillsbury. He is the only man in Rams history to be on the books of two teams at the same time as he was playing for both the Rams and Cambridge University at the time of his callup.

ONE OF THE GREATS

Tommy Cooper was a right-back of such quality that he regularly featured in lists of the greatest players to turn out for Derby County. He was capped 15 times for England before signing for Liverpool. Ironically, he became a wartime casualty while serving with the King's (Liverpool) Regiment, not on some foreign field of war but in a motorcycle accident in Suffolk where he was deployed as a dispatch rider.

THE LONG ARM OF THE KEEPER

The Rams knew that they had to keep the right side of the law when they signed Ray Middleton from Chesterfield. The goalkeeper was an active Justice of the Peace. According to sources, he was the only professional footballer to double as a magistrate.

100 AND OUT

For Jack Stamps it was a case of one hundred and out. Stamps netted his 100th league goal in the 2-1 victory away at Stoke City on April 25th 1953. He played one more game that season, and twice the following campaign, without finding the back of the net, before ending his playing career with the Rams.

LONGEST TOP FLIGHT SPELL

After a gradual decline from winning the FA Cup, the Rams were relegated from Division One at the end of the 1952/53 campaign. They had completed 20 seasons in the top flight – their longest unbroken run at the top level.

FOURTH IN A ROW

When Tim Ward took over as Rams boss, he was the fourth consecutive ex-player to become Derby County manager. In order, the three previous occupants were Stuart McMillan, Jack Barker, and Harry Storer.

OH DEAR!

Arguably the biggest shock in Derby County club history occurred on December 10th 1955 as the Rams lost 6-1 at home in the FA Cup to non-league Boston United. There were no less than six former Derby players in the victorious Boston side including Geoff Hazledine, who helped himself to a hat-trick on the day.

HELLO DIVISION THREE

The 1954/55 season was a low watermark for the Rams as they found themselves forced to play their football outside the top two divisions for the first time. The fact that the side had failed to find the back of the net 15 times during the campaign, and that the joint leading scorers had both only managed eight goals, told much of the story.

GOAL FREE

Only fans of Halifax Town and Accrington Stanley would have come away from their home games against the 1956/57 Division Three (North) championship-winning Derby County side wondering what the fuss was all about, as they were the only two hosts to keep clean sheets. Only three games in total ended with the Rams shut out. Bradford City were the only team to visit the Baseball Ground and achieve such a feat.

FALSE DAWN

Forever capable of giving supporters false hope, the Rams appeared to have turned a corner during their 1954/55 relegation campaign as they well and truly dismantled Port Vale 6-1 on February 5th. It proved to be their last victory until the final match of the season by which time they were well and truly sunk and knew that they would start the next campaign in the third tier for the first time in their history.

WINS OF STRAW

Derby County's Division Three (North) promotion season supplied supporters with another goalscoring hero, going by the name of Ray Straw. The forward had found the target 14 times the previous season, but there was nothing to suggest what was to come. In fact, it took Straw four matches to find the back of the net, but once he had started there was no stopping him and he ended the campaign with a record-equalling 37 league goals.

100 OR BUST

The first season in Division Three (North) may have ended in the ultimate disappointment of failure to gain promotion, but it was certainly entertaining as a 46-match campaign allowed the Rams to pass the 100 goals scored mark. The record-breaking total was 110.

TOP TEN APPEARANCES – 5. JACK PARRY

Jack Parry's career at Derby County spanned some 16 years and saw him bring up two milestones that only a handful of other players have achieved in the club's history. He became, at the time, only the third player to have made more than 500 appearances in a Derby shirt, following on from Steve Bloomer and Jimmy Methven in the club's early days. In total he made 517 appearances, taking into account all competitions, and in the league he racked up 483 – beaten only by Kevin Hector, who played 486 league games in his overall total of 589. Jack also finished his Derby career with 110 goals and is one of just three players to have reached a century of goals, as well as bringing up 500 appearances. The other two are Hector and Steve Bloomer, so Jack is certainly in exalted company and although he played in what was a pretty flat spell in the club's history, he can certainly be regarded as one of the best players to have ever graced the Baseball Ground. Jack spent his entire professional football career with Derby County and arrived at the club with the glow of the 1946 FA Cup win still evident. They finished third in the First Division in 1949 and reached the quarter-final of the FA Cup, then hit the same stage of the competition in 1950, as Jack's career at the Baseball Ground got off to a good start. Known as a scheming inside-forward, he was a good goalscorer but was also one of those players with so much more to his game than simply putting the ball in the back of the net. Jack had the ability to create goals as well as score them and following on from two relegations, he was at the heart of everything as the Rams scored a century of league goals in a season for the first time in 1956. That wasn't enough to earn them promotion back to the Second Division but they matched the feat again in 1957 and this time did go up, with Jack scoring regularly while also creating plenty for Ray Straw to equal the individual record of 37 league goals in a single campaign. Jack was born in Derby and although he later played for Boston United, he only ever turned out professionally for his home-town club, and as a local was really taken to the hearts of the Baseball Ground faithful.

RULES OF SUCCESS

The rule at Derby County when winning titles seemed to be to never change a winning side. As with the first time round, only 16 players featured in the 1974/75 championship win. Roy McFarland missed most of the campaign through injury and came back for the final four matches, but taking substitute appearances into the equation no-one else featured less than 13 times.

TITLE-WINNING SQUAD

The full list of players to feature in the Rams' 1974/75 title win is as follows: Colin Boulton, Jeff Bourne, Peter Daniel, Roger Davies, Archie Gemmill, Kevin Hector, Alan Hinton, Francis Lee, Roy McFarland, Henry Newton, David Nish, Steve Powell, Bruce Rioch, Rod Thomas, Colin Todd, and Ron Webster.

NO X FACTOR

With the arrival of Luciano Zavagno in 2001, the Rams had been represented by a player whose surname had begun with every letter of the alphabet apart from X. Fans might argue that X was represented in a large number of games that were either Xcellent or X-rated.

JUST THE ONCE

Although you might think that the number of players to make only one appearance for the Rams has increased with the current frequent use of the loan system – along with the rule that allows a club to name seven substitutes – that is not the case. Out of the 100 named as playing only once, 68 made their sole appearance before the outbreak of World War II.

ONLY 16

When Derby County won their first Division One championship at the end of the 1971/72 season only 16 different players featured. Of those one (Frank Wignall) was sold before Christmas and three others (Tony Bailey, Steve Powell, and Jim Walker) made six starts and four substitute appearances between them. The full list of 16 is; Tony Bailey, Colin Boulton, Alan Durban, Archie Gemmill, Kevin Hector, Terry Hennessey, Alan Hinton, Roy McFarland, John McGovern, John O'Hare, Steve Powell, John Robson, Colin Todd, Jim Walker, Ron Webster, and Frank Wignall.

DOUBLE EIGHT

Only eight Derby County players in the club's history can rightly describe themselves as double champions, having taken part in both title-winning campaigns; Colin Boulton, Archie Gemmill, Kevin Hector, Alan Hinton, Roy McFarland, Steve Powell, Colin Todd, and Ron Webster.

MAN WHO BOUGHT THE KING

Fans of a certain era are quick to point out that although the Tim Ward managerial reign was not hugely successful he was responsible for signing one of the all-time greats in Kevin Hector. Ward also brought Alan Durban to the club. The Welshman, who won both promotion and a Division One championship medal in his ten years in a Derby shirt, cost a mere £10,000 when he signed from Cardiff City in 1963.

FIRST LOCAL TO 500

When Jack Parry became the third player in club history to reach 500 performances on April 17th 1965 he became the first Derby-born player to achieve the target. Steve Bloomer, who had been the first, had grown up in Derby but was born in Cradley and Jimmy Methven, the only other individual to that point to hit the total, had been brought down from Edinburgh.

THE UNEXPECTED VISITOR

There was a bizarre aftermath to the departure of Brian Clough and Peter Taylor from Derby County. The first game after the mayhem of the week was at home to Leicester City with team coach Jimmy Gordon taking charge of affairs. All eyes were on the events unfolding in the main stand, though, as Clough appeared before the game to take the applause of the crowd while chairman Sam Longson watched in horror from the directors' box. The ex-manager had borrowed a season ticket from a sympathiser and left before the game.

SIX FROM THE START

When Eddie Thomas scored in six consecutive games between August and September in 1964 he was a long way from being the only Derby County player to manage such a feat; in fact seven had managed it previously. He remains the only Ram to date to do it in his first six appearances for the club.

FEE FOR A KING

A fee of £40,000 for a player may not seem much in the current game, but when Derby County paid the sum to Bradford Park Avenue in exchange for Kevin Hector it was a club record, and seemingly a symbol of ambition by the Rams. It proved an incredible purchase by the club given that Hector made 589 appearances, including eight as sub, netting 201 goals in the process.

BERNIE THE BOLT

Derby County have made a habit of signing high quality goalkeepers such as Colin Boulton, Mart Poom and Peter Shilton, to name but three, and it is Boulton who has made more appearances for the club than any other custodian. Signed from Cheltenham Town, he played 344 times for the Rams including every game in both of the championship-winning seasons.

CLOUGH'S FIRST CAMPAIGN

There is no doubt that the entire club underwent a whirlwind transformation upon the arrival of Brian Clough, but it is often forgotten that his effect was not instantaneous, and the Rams actually finished one place lower in the league at the end of his first season in charge than they had the campaign before.

THE £75,000 TRIO

As a symbol of what was to come during the Brian Clough era – the Rams, new manager quickly bolstered his squad with three new players. They were John O'Hare, Roy McFarland and Alan Hinton. The trio cost a grand total of £75,000 and played 1,154 times for the club between them.

SEMI SUCCESSFUL

Although league form and final position in Brian Clough's first season showed no improvement on the previous campaign, the club did reach the semi-finals of the League Cup for the first time in their history. It is a stage that they have only reached on one occasion subsequently. Ironically, it was Brian's son Nigel who was in charge when it next happened, although it was Paul Jewell who had masterminded the charge to the semis this time, only being replaced by Nigel on the night of the first leg of the semi-finals against Manchester United.

TEN GREAT HOME MATCHES – DERBY 2 ROTHERHAM 1

Two years in the third tier could be over dependent on the outcome of the visit of Rotherham to the Baseball Ground on May 9th 1986. The Rams had put in all the hard work during the first two-thirds of the season, but then endured a wobble during the run-in. Four games without a win was ended with a 3-0 victory away at Swansea City. The pressure was now on to finish the job without taking the issue to the very last game of the campaign away at Darlington and 21,036 spectators were crammed into the Baseball Ground. It was by some considerable margin the largest crowd at home for a league fixture during the whole two years in the division.

Rotherham may have been a mid-table side but that made little difference to Derby who could feel the tension inside the ground and see the finishing line just in sight. The Millers made life difficult for the hosts. It was pretty much one-way traffic for three-quarters of the contest with the Rams launching attack after attack. It could have been that the home players were getting in each other's way as they kept their opponents penned in and around their own penalty area. Mark Wallington in the home goal had very little to do for much of the game, although that was partially down to the wayward finishing of the Rotherham United strikers. The Rams should have taken the lead shortly after the restart but what seemed a clear penalty to everyone in the ground when Jeff Chandler was upended in the box was ignored by referee Fitzharris. A debut goal for Phil Gee on 77 minutes gave the hosts the lead that much of their play had deserved – a combination of Ross MacLaren and Trevor Christie providing the opening. Hardly had the Rams had a chance to take in the significance of the scoreline and Rotherham were back on level terms. The visitors had been racking up the bookings during the game, and it proved doubly disastrous for them when the already yellow carded John Dungworth tripped Bobby Davison.

The foul meant Dungworth had to go and the ensuing free kick taken by MacLaren led to a penalty appeal, this time given, for a foul on Chandler. It was all about nerve, and Trevor Christie kept his to fire Derby once more into the driving seat. This time there was no slip-up and the Rams were back in Division Two.

GREAT FINISH

The Rams won promotion to the top flight by a tidy margin when they went up under Brian Clough and Peter Taylor. In the days when two points were awarded for a win they finished seven points ahead of their nearest rivals, partially due to a tremendous finish to the campaign. They won their final nine matches – a record for consecutive wins that has yet to be beaten.

1969 PROMOTION TABLE

The top end of the final league table for the Rams' promotion-winning season of 1968/69 shows how far ahead of the rest they were. It was still two points for a win back then. Nowadays, the tally would have been 89.

	P	W	D	L	F	A	Pts
Derby County	42	26	11	5	65	32	63
Crystal Palace	42	22	12	8	70	47	56
Charlton Athletic	42	18	14	10	61	52	50
Middlesbrough	42	19	11	12	58	49	49
Cardiff City	42	20	7	15	67	54	47
Huddersfield Town	42	17	12	13	53	46	46

MACKAY'S CHANGE OF PLAN

Dave Mackay had probably assumed that a return to his first club Heart of Midlothian would make for a gentle wind-down to a career that had been filled with success. His plans were railroaded when Brian Clough talked him into joining his Derby County side in their promotion push. The decision to come to the Baseball Ground provided the Scotsman with a swansong he would never have thought possible.

THE LEY STAND

To celebrate their return to the top flight after a gap of 16 years, the Derby County board decided that an increase in capacity was called for and built the Ley Stand above the Pop Side. It proved an intelligent decision as crowds did increase, on occasion quite dramatically, with the return of top flight football to the town.

FOOTBALLER OF THE YEAR

Dave Mackay's arrival at Derby proved so successful that he ended the campaign voted Footballer of the Year by the Football Writers' Association. For the only time in the history of the award it was shared, with Tony Book of Manchester City the joint custodian. The recipient was also, usually, playing for a top division club at the time rather than leading a side to promotion.

BIGGEST BBG CROWD

The Rams set their all-time attendance record on September 20th 1969 with the visit of Tottenham Hotspur. Spurs were still considered a big side, even though past their best, that had seen them win the league and cup double earlier in the decade. With the added ingredient of it being Dave Mackay's previous club, it is not hard to see why it attracted 41,826 spectators. Given that the current capacity of Pride Park is more than 6,000 lower than that total makes for a record that is unlikely to be beaten.

WHAT A RUN

The 5-0 win over Tottenham Hotspur on September 27th 1969 saw the final victory of an incredible sequence. Starting with a 3-2 win away at Blackpool on March 8th 1969, the Rams went a phenomenal 22 consecutive league matches without tasting defeat.

EUROPE NO GO

A fourth-place finish in their first season back in the top flight for the Rams in 1970 left them in one of the qualifying spots for the following season's Uefa Cup competition. Unfortunately, the football authorities had discovered administrative irregularities at Derby County and as a punishment they were denied entry into European football that term.

FIRST £100,000 PLAYER

The first-ever Derby player to cost £100,000 was Terry Hennessey. Although it is not a sum of money in footballing terms to even blink at these days, in 1970 it was a considerable amount and spending it was considered a statement of intent by many. Hennessey played 82 times for the club in total, including three substitute appearances, and would undoubtedly have played more but for injury.

A PROMISE FULFILLED

When Brian Clough signed Roy McFarland for Derby he promised the youngster that he would play for his country, and so it proved. The centre-half gained his first full cap in February 1971, and in so doing became the first Rams player to be capped by England in over 20 years.

27 FOR WALES

When Alan Durban lined up for Wales against Northern Ireland on May 27th 1972 it was his final international cap. It meant that he had finished playing for his country as the most capped international in Rams history up to that point. His final tally was 27 caps.

TOO MUCH TO PAY?

If Derby County had seemed lavish when paying £100,000 for Terry Hennessey they smashed that amount by spending £170,000 on Colin Todd in February 1971. The money was considered unjustifiable for a defender at the time, but Todd helped them win two championships and reach the European Cup semi-final.

THE VALUE OF THE CUP

The Texaco Cup may never have been considered a prestigious competition to participate in, but it provided a young Steve Powell with the opportunity to make a first-team debut, and in the process become the youngest-ever Derby County debutant to that point. At the time of the match against Stoke City, Powell was 16 years and 30 days.

HECTOR'S HUNDRED

A fourth-round FA Cup victory at home to Notts County on February 5th 1972 may have been expected, but the 6-0 scoreline allowed Kevin Hector to score goal number 100 of his Derby County career. It was, though, only a stepping stone in an impressive Rams career.

NOT ONLY BUT ALSO

Although the first title win was a wonderful achievement for a club that had come a long way in such a small space of time, the club was strong throughout as the reserves won the Central League again while the seniors also picked up the Texaco Cup.

THE HAUNTING

A group from the Prince's Trust raising charity funds via a sleep over at Pride Park in 2007 discovered something they were not expecting. The volunteers spent the night in the cells used on matchdays for dealing with troublemakers in the bowels of the stadium. In the early hours of the morning some of the party were awoken by a rush of air as an invisible being brushed past them. A quick head count revealed that all those who should be present were still in the cells, leaving all convinced that they had discovered that the stadium was haunted.

WHAT A COMEBACK

A 1-1 draw at home to Tottenham Hotspur in the 1973 FA Cup fourth round seemed to spell the end of Derby's interest in the competition for another season, but the replay at White Hart Lane proved a classic that has been voted on occasions as the greatest-ever FA Cup match. The Rams dominated the tie but found themselves 3-1 down with only a few minutes left. Many fans left the ground and reached the railway station in time to find that their club had mounted a phenomenal comeback to win the game 5-3 with help from a Roger Davies hat-trick.

WORST-EVER TABLE

Derby County's season of shame as the worst-ever Premier League side had many lows, culminating in the earliest ever confirmed relegation in top division history. A look at the bottom end of the final table for the campaign shows just how bad it had been:

Pos.	P	W	D	L	F	A	Pts
15. Sunderland	38	11	6	21	36	59	39
16. Bolton Wanderers	38	9	10	19	36	54	37
17. Fulham	38	8	12	18	38	60	36
18. Reading	38	10	6	22	41	66	36
19. Birmingham City	38	8	11	19	46	62	35
20. Derby County	38	1	8	29	20	89	11

KING OF HAT-TRICKS

The great Steve Bloomer hit an incredible 18 hat-tricks during his time with the Rams. The nearest any Derby player has ever got to that record is Jack Bowers who managed 11 and Harry Bedford who hit ten.

ROGER'S RECORD

It is common knowledge amongst Rams fans that over the years their club has broken transfer records a number of times. Many would struggle, though, to name club legend Roger Davies amongst those record breakers. It is, however, true that the princely sum of £12,000 that the club paid to Worcester City was at the time a record fee for a player signed from a non-league club.

I PREDICT A RIOT

It is hard to imagine that the departure of a manager, no matter how popular, could lead to the kind of furore that the resignation of Brian Clough created. Protest marches and public meetings attended by hundreds of supporters showed the depth of feeling for the man who had brought success back to the club. It all proved in vain as the board of directors quickly installed Dave Mackay in the hot seat, as the only individual with the respect and charisma to prevent Derby County from totally imploding.

MACKAY BREAKS THE FALL

The club was in such disarray after the departure of Brian Clough and Peter Taylor there was every possibility of the Rams going into free fall. Mackay had been in charge for six games before managing to register his first win. His determination to get Derby back on track proved so effective, however, that the team ended the campaign in third place and qualified once again for European football.

FIVE ALIVE

The visit of Luton Town to the Baseball Ground on March 29th 1975 for a league match allowed Roger Davies to achieve something that had not been managed in over forty years. Davies scored five goals in the game and had a further two disallowed. It was the fifth time such a feat had occurred, and it has never subsequently been repeated.

THE MOST DISASTROUS INJURY

Arguably the most disastrous injury in club history was the shoulder dislocation suffered by Charlie George in a clash with Stoke City's Denis Smith in a home game on March 24th 1976. The Rams were on course for an FA Cup and league double. George had been the catalyst for much of the success that season, but after he was led off the field results slumped. Derby won just two more games that season, finishing fourth, and were dumped out of the FA Cup at the semi-final stage by Manchester United.

FIVE OR MORE

The full list of players to score five or more goals in a single game is as follows.

Alexander Higgins... 5 v Aston Villa	....	December 28th 1889
John McMillan .... 5 v Wolves	....	January 10th 1891
Steve Bloomer .... 6 v Aston Villa	....	January 21st 1899
John Moore .... 5 v Crystal Palace	....	December 25th 1922
Hugh Gallacher .... 5 v Blackburn Rovers	...	December 15th 1934
Roger Davies .... 5 v Luton Town	....	March 29th 1975
Kevin Hector .... 5 v Finn Harps	....	September 15th 1976

FIVE AWAY

Hugh Gallacher deserves special praise for his feat of hitting five goals in a single game. Only seven players have achieved the total in club history. Gallacher was the only one to hit five on the road, with his goals coming away to Blackburn Rovers.

THE EUROPEAN FIVE

Amongst the many goalscoring feats of Kevin Hector was his performance against Finn Harps on September 15th 1976. The Irish part-timers were crushed 12-0 with Hector netting five of them. Not only was that the highest number of goals by a Derby player in an individual European tie, it was the only time in club history that one individual hit five in any cup competition. Harps were founded in 1954 and hail from the tiny town of Ballyboefy in County Donegal, close to the Northern Ireland border.

TOP TEN APPEARANCES – 4. STEVE BLOOMER

There can't be many Rams fans around – if any – who saw Steve Bloomer play, but there can't be many – if any – who are not aware of what a club legend he is for Derby County. Widely regarded as football's first superstar, Steve played 525 games for Derby over two spells and scored 332 goals, a figure that nobody has ever got close to and one that is unlikely to ever be beaten. Steve was born in Cradley, in the West Midlands, but his family moved to Derby when he was young and his career with the Rams eventually began after an education locally. Although he didn't score on his competitive debut, on September 3rd 1892, he soon became as prolific as they come. Steve was Derby's leading scorer for 14 consecutive seasons, and with the club he was also the First Division's leading scorer on five occasions – 1896, 1897, 1899, 1901 and 1904, while in 1896 – jointly with Aston Villa's John Campbell – he was the leading scorer in any European league. Between 1895 and 1907 Steve also made 23 appearances for England and scored in all of his first ten international appearances, which remains a record to this day, as he racked up 19 goals. Overall he hit 28 goals in 23 international matches and became the first man to score two hat-tricks for England. With Derby, he helped the club to the FA Cup finals of 1898, 1899 and 1903, scoring in the first final against Nottingham Forest. Steve also fired Derby to the runners-up spot in the First Division in 1896 and his goals were worth the entrance fee to watch the Rams on their own. But, there was shock and anger when he joined Middlesbrough in 1906 for a fee of £750. Four years later he was persuaded back to the Baseball Ground by manager Jimmy Methven, one of his old team-mates, and helped Derby win promotion back to the First Division in 1912. He scored his 332nd and final goal for the club on September 6th 1913 against Sheffield United and played his last game the following January, 11 days after his 40th birthday. Steve's brother Philip played one game for the club but the more famous Bloomer sibling is now immortalised at Pride Park Stadium with a pitch side bust that looks out over the action. Steve died in 1938 and his grave can be found at the city's Nottingham Road cemetery.

RECORD AGGREGATE

The Rams' record aggregate victory came in September 1977 against Finn Harps in the Uefa Cup. Already 12-0 up from the home leg, Derby won the away tie 4-1 – and even managed to score the sole consolation from the head of Roy McFarland.

BLOOMER'S RECORD BROKEN

It took 62 years to break Steve Bloomer's record number of 502 appearances, but it was achieved on April 23rd 1977 by Ron Webster who went on to make a total of 535, including five from the subs' bench.

TICKER TOP

Despite being surrounded by players of international pedigree at full and Under-23 level, it was Peter Daniel, who never gained representative honours, who won the Player of the Year award at the end of the second title-winning season of 1974/75. Daniel, who played in any number of outfield positions during his career, gained the award by magnificently deputising for centre-half Roy McFarland.

WEMBLEY DEBUTANT

Charlie George was a brilliant signing for the Rams when he was brought to the club by manager Dave Mackay for the 1975/76 campaign. The defending champions played FA Cup winners West Ham United in the FA Charity Shield – the traditional curtain raiser to the season. This made George the only player to make his competitive debut for Derby at Wembley.

FIRST SCOTLAND CAPTAIN

The first Derby County player to be selected to captain Scotland was Archie Gemmill. The honour came for the little Scottish midfielder at the end of the 1975/76 season. It was the only campaign in which he was an ever-present, and his first match as on-field leader was against Wales.

HARPING ON ABOUT IT

Kevin Hector goes down in the record books as the player to inflict the most damage on a club in a single tie. In the two-legged Uefa Cup tie against Finn Harps, Hector netted five at home before adding a further brace to his tally in the away fixture.

DEJA VU

The Derby County board once again showed an incredible capacity to self-destruct when Dave Mackay and assistant Des Anderson were dismissed after a 2-0 defeat away to Everton in November 1976. The Rams had failed to register a single league win until the ninth game of the campaign, and only managed two wins before Mackay's departure; it meant that both league title-winning managers had been forced out within 18 months of lifting the championship.

THE RETURN OF THE KING

In February 1977 the unthinkable seemed to be about to happen. Brian Clough was to return triumphantly to the Baseball Ground and continue where he had left off. That at least was the theory. Somewhere between the negotiations and the announcement Clough changed his mind, and when he actually arrived at the press conference he only confirmed that he wasn't in fact coming back at all.

REIGN IN SPAIN

The Rams celebrated their first Football League title win while on holiday. Nowadays, all matches must be completed before the nominated last day of the season, but in the 1970s a few rearranged games spilled over beyond the supposed last date. Derby played their final fixture (a 1-0 home win over Liverpool) before jetting away on a team holiday. So it was that they were all abroad together when news came through that the only teams capable of overtaking them – Leeds United and Liverpool – had failed to do so and they were champions.

TABLE-TOPPING FINISH

The top of the final table for the first Derby County title-winning campaign looked like this:

	P	W	D	L	F	A	Pts
Derby County	42	24	10	8	69	33	58
Leeds United	42	24	9	9	73	31	57
Liverpool	42	24	9	9	64	30	57
Manchester City	42	23	11	8	77	45	57
Arsenal	42	22	8	12	58	40	52
Tottenham	42	19	13	10	63	42	51

BETTER THAN EXPECTED

The revolving door policy introduced by Tommy Docherty when he took over at Derby County unsurprisingly made for inconsistent performances. The club still managed to finish 12th despite only managing a maximum of two consecutive wins three times after Docherty's arrival.

CHOPPING DOWN THE FOREST

The undoubted high spot of the 1979/80 season was the comprehensive 4-1 victory over local rivals Nottingham Forest. If fans thought that a corner had been turned with such a morale-boosting win, they were sadly disappointed as the team failed to pick up another victory in the next 12 games. Unsurprisingly, the Rams ended the campaign relegated.

SPURRED ON TO VICTORY

The biggest league victory of modern times came in Dave Mackay's penultimate win as Rams manager. His side had gone eight games from the start of the season without a single win before the visit of Tottenham Hotspur to the Baseball Ground. A patched-up Derby County side, with Bruce Rioch pressed into duty as a striker, won 8-2 in a game that featured one of only two goals scored for the club by Welsh international defender Rod Thomas.

WE ARE THE CHAMPIONS

The top of the final table for the second Derby County league title was as follows:

	P	W	D	L	F	A	Pts
Derby County	42	21	11	10	67	49	53
Liverpool	42	20	11	11	60	39	51
Ipswich Town	42	23	5	14	66	44	51
Everton	42	16	18	8	56	42	50
Stoke City	42	17	15	10	64	48	49
Sheffield United	42	18	13	11	58	51	49
Middlesbrough	42	18	12	12	54	40	48
Manchester City	42	18	10	14	54	54	46
Leeds United	42	16	16	13	57	49	45

FIRST PENALTY SHOOT-OUT

The Rams' first experience of penalty shoot-outs came on November 6th 1974. The match was a Uefa Cup tie against Atletico Madrid. The aggregate score was 4-4 and Derby came back from Spain winners thanks to triumphing 7-6 on penalties.

A SPOT OF HEARTBREAK

Derby County's first domestic penalty shoot-out ended in heartbreak. Drawn against Queens Park Rangers in the League Cup, the Rams held out for a 0-0 draw at Loftus Road, but could do no better in the replay at the Baseball Ground. The tie was still scoreless after 210 minutes of football. Derby proceeded to lose the ensuing penalty shoot-out 5-3 in front of their own fans.

FIRST SINCE THE KING

When Bobby Davison netted 24 league goals in the 1984/85 campaign he became the first player to pass 20 league goals in a single season since Kevin Hector in 1967/68.

EAST MIDLAND WANDERERS

Gary Mills and Trevor Christie share the honour of playing for all four of the main East Midlands clubs; Derby County, Leicester City, Notts County, and Nottingham Forest. Many players have turned out for a combination of the quartet but few have a full house.

BETTER LATE THAN NEVER

Steve Buckley was a great and consistent performer for the Rams, but with a better scouting network, the club could have saved much of the £163,000 transfer fee that they paid for him. Buckley was born just over the Nottinghamshire border at a place called Brinsley and played his early football for non-league sides Ilkeston Town and Burton Albion.

WORST TREATED BOSS?

Colin Murphy is probably the worst treated manager in Derby County history. Promoted to caretaker manager from reserve-team coach, he was in charge when the directors made their ill-fated attempt to bring Brian Clough back to the club. He also took charge of his last game as manager knowing that Tommy Docherty was about to replace him.

LAST OF A BREED?

When Rams legend Roy McFarland passed the 500 appearance mark at home to Sheffield Wednesday on October 4th 1980, he became the seventh Derby player to reach that target. None have got close since then, and with the speed that players move on one wonders if he will be the last.

FAMILIAR COMPANY

Glenn Skivington only scored three Derby goals in a career of 50 games, including seven substitute appearances. The first was in a 4-1 league win over Crystal Palace, the other goals coming courtesy of Kevin Wilson and Steve Buckley. He followed that up with a strike in the 3-1 league victory over Rotherham United, with the other goals coming from Wilson and Buckley. His final goal was in a League Cup tie against Hartlepool United in 1982. Also among the goals on that occasion were – yes – Kevin Wilson and Steve Buckley.

THE BEST AWARDS NIGHT – EVER

In the 1970s, Derby County made a habit of winning major prizes when already celebrating. With games running out, Ipswich Town blew their game in hand while Derby players were celebrating their Player of the Year awards night in a local nightclub. The news that they were champions again only helped to improve the already celebratory atmosphere.

RETURN OF THE KING

Rated as surplus to requirements by Tommy Docherty, Rams legend Kevin Hector left the club only to return to a hero's welcome when brought back by Colin Addison. The move allowed Hector the opportunity to break the 200-goal barrier for the club – which he duly managed in a League Cup tie against West Ham United on October 7th 1981.

THE ILLEGAL APPROACH

Derby County have frequently courted controversy and they found themselves in trouble again when new manager Peter Taylor decided to bring Roy McFarland back to the club as his assistant. McFarland had left County to carve out a career in management as player-manager at Bradford City, a role that he found himself doing well. Unfortunately, the Derby approach for him was deemed illegal and the club were fined.

HOWARD'S OLD TRAFFORD HIGHLIGHT

Steve Howard was the epitome of a journeyman footballer. He worked his way up from non-league Tow Law Town, through the lower divisions of the Football League, and found himself in the Premier League with Derby after leading the line in the 2006/07 promotion campaign. Goalscoring at the top level proved hard not just for Steve, but the entire team. He scored just one Premier League goal for the Rams, away to Manchester United. It was one of only seven league goals United conceded at home during the entire season.

THERE AND BACK AGAIN

It seems a common feature of Derby County history that when times have been bad the club has invited old heroes to return to put things right. A partial list of such players would include Steve Bloomer, Kevin Hector, Archie Gemmill, Bobby Davison, and Charlie George. So far, the only manager to return has been Peter Taylor, though he was only assistant first time round.

THE BEST RELEGATION

Relegation would not normally be seen as a sign of success at a football club, but when the Rams were relegated at the end of the 1983/84 season it was still an achievement. Derby County had been the subject of a winding-up petition from the Inland Revenue for much of the campaign. The matter was resolved in April 1984 and although the club went down at least it was still in existence.

THE MAN WITH NO TEAM

When Arthur Cox took over the managerial reins at recently-relegated Derby County he did not have enough senior players to field a full 11-man team. By scouring the market for free transfers and loan signings he started to fashion a side. Such was his managerial acumen that the decline was arrested and the club finished seventh in Division Three.

THE DOUBLE CENTURION

Steve Buckley was the best signing that Tommy Docherty made while in charge of the Rams. A model of consistency, he is the only player in club history to have passed a century of consecutive appearances twice.

HERO TO ZERO (2)

Steve Cherry was a more than adequate goalkeeper. The fact that he played 90 games for the first team is testament to that. Sadly for many fans the abiding memory will be of him flapping a corner into the back of his own net in a sixth-round FA Cup tie against Plymouth Argyle, denying the Rams a lucrative semi-final appearance. Particularly galling for Cherry would be the knowledge that but for heroics from him in the first game there probably would have been no replay.

MORE VALUABLE WHEN SOLD

As a goalscorer Kevin Wilson was of value to his team; he netted 41 goals in 141 appearances. His value to the team was even more significant after he was sold to Ipswich Town for £150,000. The money realised from the sale allowed Rams boss Arthur Cox to bring in Trevor Christie, Gary Micklewhite and Geraint Williams, who all played important roles in getting the club back to the top flight.

NOT HIS BEST

The 1987/88 Division One campaign was the first real reverse suffered by the Rams under the management of Arthur Cox as the side lost eight games consecutively, equalling their worst-ever run.

OUT THE WINDOW

John Burridge was a goalkeeper who played for a number of clubs throughout his career. A dedicated professional, it was unsurprising when Arthur Cox brought the player in on loan during his first season as manager. Cox was so keen to sign the player on a permanent basis that he locked him in a room at the Raynesway training ground until he agreed. Burridge made his escape by climbing though a window and the Derby boss failed to get his man.

NO TIME TO STOP

As they had done in the 1950s, the Rams earned promotion from the third tier at the second time of asking at the end of the 1985/86 campaign. Arthur Cox had done such a good job that not only did the seniors gain promotion but the reserves became the first-ever side from the Third Division to do so.

LEST WE FORGET

For many supporters Robert Maxwell was the most reviled name in club history. If it were not for Maxwell and the efforts of Stuart Webb there would have been no club whatsoever. The Rams found themselves in a dreadful financial state. Webb persuaded Maxwell to put his financial power behind the club, and though it took more than one trip to the High Court to settle debts it was the money of Robert Maxwell that kept the club alive.

HOW WRONG CAN YOU BE

Some supporters felt that much needed to be done to their side after Arthur Cox had dragged them out of Division Three in third place. They felt their worst fears had been confirmed when they lost the opening game of the season 1-0 at home to Oldham Athletic. It was the last home defeat of the entire campaign, however.

12TH MAN WINS THE GAME

Managers often refer to the crowd as 'the 12th man'. Never was this shown more than on May 9th 1987. The Rams were 2-1 down at home to Plymouth Argyle in the last match of the season. If Portsmouth won their game they would be promoted as champions. News started to filter round the Baseball Ground of the current state of the other match. As a chant of 'Portsmouth are losing' started the Rams lifted their performance. Derby went on to win 4-2 and clinch promotion as champions.

THE LONGEST MILE

When the fixture list for the 2009/10 season came out Rams fans' hearts dropped when they saw that the computer had provided them with a Tuesday night trip to Plymouth. The Devon club represents, by some considerable distance, the longest journey that Derby County have ever faced for a league game. The minimum mileage possible there and back is 498 miles.

WE'VE LOST THAT LOSING FEELING

The Rams clearly lost the losing habit during the 1986/87 promotion campaign. Not only did they remain undefeated at home after the opening-day fixture, they were undefeated in the league anywhere between January 24th and April 11th, a run of 13 matches.

COX'S UNIQUE RECORD

Arthur Cox may have inherited a mess when he became Rams manager but he was so successful that he became the only Derby boss to earn two consecutive promotions. Thankfully, the years spent in the third tier have been mercifully short, thus denying others the opportunity to equal his feat.

CASE FOR THE DEFENCE

A need to strengthen the defence for Derby's return to the top flight under Arthur Cox resulted in the signing of Peter Shilton and Mark Wright for the 1987/88 season. Wright cost £760,000 and broke a transfer fee record that had stood for seven years.

SKIPPER SHILTS

As the senior man in the squad, Peter Shilton had the honour of wearing the captain's armband during the 1990 World Cup finals. In doing so he became the first Ram to lead an England side in the most prestigious of football tournaments.

MISSING OUT ON EUROPE

At the end of the 1988/89 season the Rams again found themselves finishing high enough in the league to qualify for European football for the first time since 1976. English clubs were, however, banned from European competitions at the time after the Heysel Stadium tragedy in 1985.

DEAN DEAL INSPIRED

The signing of Dean Saunders from Oxford United proved a master-stroke by Arthur Cox. Saunders excited the crowd by scoring twice on his debut against Wimbledon and found the back of the net on each of his first four appearances. More than that, for Derby supporters, was the knowledge that he was the first £1m signing in club history.

ENGLAND'S NUMBER ONE

Peter Shilton ended his international career while at Derby County. He gained 34 caps while with the club, making him the most capped player in Rams history at that point. Even more impressively, it meant that Shilton retired as England's most-capped player ever with 125 caps.

TOP TEN APPEARANCES – 3. ROY MCFARLAND

There isn't much that Roy McFarland hasn't achieved while connected to Derby County in a career with the club that began in 1967 and ended in 1995. He was signed from Tranmere Rovers as a raw 19-year-old by Brian Clough and Peter Taylor, who promised to turn him into the best centre-half in England. They delivered. Roy was already showing plenty of potential in a Derby shirt by the time the legendary Dave Mackay arrived in 1968 and slotted in at the back alongside his younger colleague. Derby marched to promotion in 1968/69, with Roy at the heart of the defence, to win the club's inaugural Player of the Year award, and he made the transition to First Division football with ease. Roy then became an England international in 1971 and is regarded as one of the country's finest post-war defenders, although 28 caps was no reward for his immense ability. In 1971/72, he captained Derby to their first-ever league title and stepped on to the European stage the following season, scoring in the memorable win over Benfica at the Baseball Ground, though he was controversially suspended for the second leg of the semi-final against Juventus. Derby were again champions in 1974/75, but Roy was cruelly ruled out of all but the final four games by an Achilles tendon injury collected while on duty with England, although he made a triumphant return and then scored at Wembley in the Charity Shield at the start of the following season. Roy took his Baseball Ground playing career into a third different decade by lining up until 1981, when he called time on life at Derby to take up the player-manager role at Bradford City. He returned to the Rams a year later, having won promotion with the Bantams, and had his boots on again in 1983/84 for eight final appearances for a total of 530, along with a spell as caretaker manager, before reverting to assistant boss under Arthur Cox. Roy was at Cox's side in the successive promotions to the top flight before taking over in 1993, guiding the team to sixth in that first season and a heartbreaking defeat to Leicester City at Wembley in the play-off final. He left at the end of the 1994/95 season and remains settled in Derby where he is regularly seen at games. Roy's last act as a football manager was to guide Burton Albion over the line to the Football League in 2009 after taking over when Nigel Clough left to join Derby.

A RECORD EXIT

Paul Goddard formed a great strike partnership with Dean Saunders during their time at Derby County. To the surprise of fans, Goddard was sold to Millwall in December 1989. His departure did provide the Rams with a fee of £800,000 – the largest received to that point.

MONEY ISN'T EVERYTHING

If Derby fans thought that having a multi-millionaire in Robert Maxwell as a chairman and owner meant that the club could compete with the big boys on level terms, they clearly had no idea of the state of Maxwell's finances. The Rams suddenly found themselves more involved in selling than buying. The club was relegated at the end of the 1990/91 campaign. The sale of Dean Saunders to Liverpool for £2.9m did give the club a new record fee for a transfer out.

NOT FOUR-MIDABLE

Scoring four goals at home would seem a guarantee of victory but, incredibly, on December 15th 1990, Derby County contrived to lose 6-4 to visitors Chelsea. It was the beginning of the end for the team as the Rams went on a record-breaking run of 20 games without a win. Unsurprisingly, they were relegated by the end of the campaign.

BERNARD VANN VC

Bernard Vann is the only former Ram to be awarded the Victoria Cross. He played three games as an amateur and after taking Holy Orders sought permission from the Bishop of Peterborough to join the Sherwood Foresters in World War I. For his courage he was also awarded the Military Cross with Bar and the French Croix DeGuerre with Palm Leaves.

ARTHUR'S KIND MOVE

When Bobby Davison left Derby to join Leeds United he was two goals shy of a century. Luckily Arthur Cox chose to bring him back on loan to aid the Rams' promotion push. He played ten games, scoring eight goals in the process, and although the club dipped out on an immediate return to the top flight, Davison at least broke the 100-goals mark for the club.

CHOPPER GETS THE CHOP

There can be no doubt that Robert Maxwell was the most colourful chairman that the Rams ever had. A larger than life character, he was not universally popular with the fans, especially after he tightened the purse strings and turned a buying club into a selling one. On one famous occasion, he arrived at a home game by helicopter to join the team photograph, and flew away at half-time. While telling the pilot how popular he was because of all the fans waving him goodbye he seemed blissfully unaware that most of those waving were doing so with only two fingers.

LIONEL'S RECORD-BREAKERS

Once local businessman Lionel Pickering had taken over the ownership of Derby County he was so eager for success that the club twice broke its record for transfers in less than a fortnight. The Rams first brought Paul Kitson in from Leicester City in a player exchange deal rated at £1.3m, and shortly thereafter Tommy Johnson was added to the squad for a fee of £1.375m, which was paid to Notts County.

BLOOMER ON FILM

With Steve Bloomer having finished playing for the Rams in the early years of the 20th century, it is fair to say that no-one reading this will ever have seen him play. In fact very few people will know what he looks like from anything other than old black and white photographs. There exists, incredibly, moving images of Bloomer. Sadly, the film is not of him playing football but departing by boat to go and coach the Canadian Army football team. The footage belongs to British Pathé and at the time of writing was available for viewing by anyone interested on YouTube.

A LONG OLD SEASON

The 1992/93 season provided the Rams with a record high number of games. Lengthy runs in both the FA and League cups were combined with success in the Anglo-Italian Cup. Derby County made it all the way to the Wembley final where they faced US Cremonese. This added a further nine games onto their domestic schedule, making for a grand total of 64 matches in all competitions.

TEN GREAT HOME MATCHES – DERBY 4 PLYMOUTH 2

Twelve months after hauling themselves out of Division Three, the Rams found themselves once again on the promotion trail. Unlike the campaign before when they had made it as third-placed side in the years before play-offs, this time they had kept the momentum of the previous campaign going and for a good while before the season ended it had been a question of whether they would go up as champions, or in second place, with Portsmouth occupying the other spot. Arthur Cox's men had been consistently in the top two positions since the middle of January but it was so tight that the title was not to be decided until the last day. Derby were at home to Plymouth Argyle while Portsmouth hosted Sheffield United. Nerves seemed to get the better of the Rams who struggled to put together much by way of passing play and managed to shoot themselves in the foot by conceding within the first ten minutes. Half-time arrived with the title seemingly destined for Fratton Park. Portsmouth were a goal up and the Rams were one down. What happened in the second half will live long in Derby legend. Sheffield United clawed their way back into the game on the south coast, and as news filtered through to the Baseball Ground fans started to chant that Portsmouth were losing. The effect galvanised the home side. Bobby Davison gave his team a way back into the contest with a superb left-foot strike. Back came Plymouth, but when a free kick given on the edge of the Derby box was cleared to Nigel Callaghan, the winger ran half the length of the park to put Derby two goals to the good.

The game looked to be over a minute later as this time Callaghan turned provider, playing in a pass that was converted by Gary Micklewhite after Steve Cherry in the Plymouth goal could only parry the ball. Derby never make life easy for themselves, however, and with four minutes remaining Argyle pulled a goal back once again through Garry Nelson. Determined not to let things slip at this stage, the Rams kept pressing forward and got their reward on the stroke of full time with John Gregory finishing off the campaign in true captain's style by completing good work by Davison by nearly breaking the net with his shot. The second biggest crowd of the league season, 20,798, had seen their team win 4-2 and gain promotion as champions.

RAMS BREAK NEW GROUND

Derby County were one of the first clubs in the country to set up matchday commentary, especially for hospital patients, and the blind and partially sighted supporters in the ground. Portsmouth were the very first and Derby started their service a few weeks into the 1952/53 season after being given professional training by BBC personnel. Bertie Mee, who went on to lead Arsenal to the league and cup double, was one of the first commentators for the Rams while one of his colleagues, a local teacher who specialised in history named Roy Christian, was with the service from the start for 50 years until retiring as probably the longest-serving sports commentator in the world.

SPLASHING THE CASH

If fans thought Arthur Cox was pushing the boat out when he paid more than £1.3m twice in ten days they were staggered to see the transfer record comprehensively smashed in September 1993. Needing a dominant centre-half, Cox once again went to Notts County, this time buying Craig Short for a staggering £2.65m.

REPORTER'S SHORT NOTES

So impressive was Craig Short in his final season with the Rams that he was voted Player of the Year by supporters. One tabloid journalist dispatched to the last home league game of the 1994/95 campaign against Southend built his entire match report around the award, before detailing Short's dominant display in the air, on the ground, and as an all-round on-field leader during the game which Derby lost 2-1. It is just a shame that the reporter had not questioned local reporters or even checked his team sheet, or he might have realised that Short was suspended and therefore unavailable to play!

FROM DESK TO DUGOUT

Jim Smith thought his days at the sharp end of football were over after his experiences at Portsmouth. Resigned to a desk job with the League Managers' Association he leapt at the chance to run a team again. It proved an inspired appointment as Smith joined the elite few to have led a Derby County side to promotion in their first full season at the helm.

BOSSES ARE OUTSIDERS

Derby County have been employing managers in the modern sense – that is a man responsible for picking the team and team affairs – since 1906. At the time of writing there have been 26 different full-time managers of the club, but there has yet to be a single one born inside the county boundary. The nearest to date has been Peter Taylor who was born over the border in Nottingham.

A LONG CLIMB

If anyone had a right to believe that footballers have it easy it was Martin Taylor. The goalkeeper worked his way up from non-league Mile Oak Rovers, and knew what real life was all about as he was employed as an apprentice miner before joining the ranks of full-time footballers.

JEEPERS KEEPERS

April 20th 1991 saw the Rams travel to Maine Road for a do-or-die match against Manchester City. Derby lost the game but a piece of history was made on the day. In the opposing goals were Martin Taylor for Derby and Tony Cotton for City. The two keepers had both started their careers at non-league Mile Oak Rovers, and the match represented the first time that two former non-league goalkeepers had faced each other in a top division game.

NON-LEAGUE SHOPPING

Over the years Derby County have brought a number of players straight out of non-league into the squad. Among those who have made the step up are: Roger Davies, Kevin Wilson, Martin Taylor, Ben Pringle, Dick Pratley, Kevin Francis, David Penney, Frank Gamble, Tony Bailey, and Colin Boulton.

FRANK A GAMBLE

Frank Gamble's good fortune was to be plucked from non-league Burscough to join Second Division Derby County. His misfortune was to get his break while the club was in crisis. The early 1980s saw the club in free fall and with a mounting financial disaster looming. Gamble made seven appearances and scored two goals before talking to a tabloid journalist about all the problems that Derby faced and turning his back on a career in league football.

PAULO'S SOLO STUNNER

It was voted the best goal in Rams' history, which is almost impossible to judge, given all the goals scored over the years. Certainly, the solo effort by Paulo Wanchope on his debut at Old Trafford has to go down as one of the most spectacular first efforts for Derby County down the years.

RAMS ON THE ROAD

If good form on the road is a major factor in a successful season the Rams should have walked the league in 1991/92. They broke their own record for the number of away wins, returning home with all the points on 12 occasions. They ended the campaign two points shy of the automatic promotion places and were then knocked out in the play-offs.

COX'S AWAY DOUBLE

Away form under Arthur Cox certainly showed a major improvement over what had gone before. His team twice broke the record of number of away league victories in a single campaign and during the 1992/93 season embarked on a run of seven consecutive away victories – yet another club record.

HARKES AT THAT

The first player to represent his country while on the books of Derby County from outside the British Isles was John Harkes. The midfielder played for the United States in the 1994 World Cup finals on their own soil. It was the first time in the club's 110-year history that this had happened. Harkes went on to make 90 appearances for his country, scoring on six occasions.

TAYLOR'S ROLLERCOASTER

If the 1993/94 season was a personal triumph for Martin Taylor, who was an ever-present and also voted Player of the Season, the following campaign was mired in tragedy for the goalkeeper who suffered a horrific double fracture of the leg in a clash with Dave Regis at Southend on October 16th 1994. Although Taylor fought his way back and did make a handful of appearances for the Rams in the Premiership he was out of the game for 29 months. Taylor had been so consistent before the injury there were suggestions that he was on the verge of an England call-up when it happened.

TEN GREAT HOME MATCHES – DERBY 3 ARSENAL 0

The Rams had only been back in the Premier League since the summer of 1996, and had only been at the new Pride Park Stadium for a matter of months, before they really announced themselves as a side to be reckoned with thanks to this result. Arsenal, the last opposing team to win at the Baseball Ground, travelled north unbeaten so far in the Premier League and would have fancied their chances of becoming the first winners at Pride Park. They were in the early days of the Arsene Wenger era but the man in the Rams hotseat would have the last laugh. Before the game, Jim Smith had been presented with a new set of golf clubs to mark his 25 years in football management. Also ahead of kick-off, Paulo Wanchope had been presented with the Carling No. 1 award for his performances as the Premier League's star player in September. Wanchope would go on to have a major say in the outcome of this game in front of a crowd of over 30,000. Arsenal had the better of the first half and should have been ahead but Ian Wright hammered a penalty against the crossbar and Nicolas Anelka headed the rebound over. Derby had defended solidly before the break and a tactical switch at half-time paid dividends in the second period. Within a couple of minutes of the restart, Wanchope embarked on one of his trademark loping runs forward and got to the edge of the box before letting his shot go. He didn't make a great contact but it was accurate enough to beat David Seaman and find the bottom corner. The Costa Rican nearly fluffed another good chance before, on 66 minutes, putting Derby 2-0 ahead from close range after poor defensive work from Nigel Winterburn. The Rams' third goal was their best of the afternoon, a neat pass from Francesco Baiano sending Dean Sturridge racing away for a classy finish over the advancing Seaman to wrap up what was a memorable win. It was a result that Derby more than deserved as they made the rest of the top flight sit up and take notice of how they had brushed aside the Gunners, who returned to London with their tails between their legs after being beaten for the first time that season. What made the afternoon stand out even more was Arsenal, in their first full season under Wenger, then going on to win the Double.

DAILLY DEAL

When Jim Smith signed Christian Dailly from Dundee United – although he may have been unsure whether he had signed a midfielder or a defender – in 1996 he knew he had got a jewel. Dailly was the most capped Scotland Under-21 player who went on to gain his first full caps while at Derby. Even Smith would have valued the player at less than the £5.35m that Blackburn paid for him in August 1998. The fee was a Derby County record for an outgoing player.

STEVE A KEY COG

There are a number of players brought to Derby by Jim Smith who could be described as important signings, but arguably the best that Smith signed was Steve McClaren. As a player at the club, McClaren had managed 30 starts, plus two sub appearances, but his reputation as a coach was what attracted Smith. The fact that he went on to be Sir Alex Ferguson's assistant at Manchester United and then England boss only served to confirm Smith's judgement.

IGOR! IGOR! IGOR!

If the arrival of a single player can be seen as a catalyst to success in recent times it has to be the arrival of Igor Stimac. A season of mid-table mediocrity at best seemed to be beckoning for the 1995/96 season until the arrival of the Croatian. Initial signs were not promising as the Rams lost his debut game against Tranmere Rovers 5-1, but the club then went on a 20-match unbeaten run to set the seeds for a promotion push. The run was a record for a single season.

KING'S CROWNING MOMENT

The last Derby player to score a goal at the Baseball Ground was Kevin Hector. Although used for reserve fixtures for several seasons after the club decamped to Pride Park, the final games played there were for charity including one featuring the ex-Rams. Hector, who had graced the Baseball Ground for many years, notched the final goal of the game. In a match, incidentally, in which Scott Matthews, son of one of the authors of this book, was picked as the last-ever mascot for a game at the old stadium.

FIVE IN FRANCE

The 1998 World Cup finals saw the Rams represented by the largest number of players in club history. Five players from four different countries travelled to France with varying degrees of expectation. The quintet were; Igor Stimac (Croatia), Jacob Laursen (Denmark), Deon Burton and Darryl Powell (Jamaica), and Christian Dailly (Scotland).

SIX-HITTER JIMMY

Jimmy Lyons was the first player between the two World Wars to net in six consecutive games. The run, which started on January 6th 1923, comprised of four league games and two in the FA Cup.

ENGLAND'S PRIDE

A record crowd of 32,865 greeted the first international fixture played at Pride Park. The match was played between England Under-21s and their French counterparts. When the game, which England won 2-1, was played on February 9th 1999 it was not only a Pride Park attendance record but the largest crowd to see England Under-21s anywhere in the country.

SWINGING THE AXE

Getting rid of the manager is usually a sign that things are not going well. Changing the occupant of the hotseat twice in a season suggests a crisis. For the first time in their history, the Rams had three different managers during the 2001/02 campaign. Jim Smith was in charge at the start of the season, but after his team failed to pick up a single victory after the first game he departed in October and his assistant Colin Todd took up the challenge. Todd managed just four wins in 15 Premier League matches, before another crowd favourite, John Gregory, arrived with the intention of steering the club to safety. He was unable to do it.

A FULL HOUSE

The all-time attendance record for a competitive fixture at Pride Park is 33,597. It was reached when the senior England team played a friendly against Mexico in May 2001 as Wembley was rebuilt. The lack of many travelling fans meant that the usual areas closed to aid segregation of opposing supporters could be kept open. For the record, England won 4-0 with goals from Paul Scholes, Robbie Fowler, David Beckham and Teddy Sheringham.

CRAMMING THEM IN

Liverpool has usually been a big draw when playing away to Derby County, and so it proved when the two teams met at Pride Park on March 18th 2000. A record-breaking 33,378 crowd attended the game, but the majority of them would have returned home disappointed as the Rams lost the match 2-0.

THE FUERTES SAGA

The Rams' most disastrous ever mid-season break occurred in November 1999 when Jim Smith signed Argentinean forward Esteban Fuertes. Fuertes claimed European ancestry and therefore held an Italian passport, which negated the need to go through the foreign work-permit procedure. The team flew out to Portugal for a warm-weather break during an international weekend. Unfortunately, when the club returned to England Fuertes was denied entry into the country as his Italian passport was apparently forged. As a result Fuertes was put on the first plane back to Argentina. The Rams got their money back the following summer by transferring the player to RC Lens. The striker had played eight league games and scored one goal by the time the deception was uncovered.

GREGORY ON THE GO

Managers have come and gone from Derby County over the years. Some have moved on to other clubs, while others have been dismissed for lack of success. John Gregory is the only boss to have been suspended, however, in 2003, with the club citing serious misconduct. Interestingly, nothing specific was ever mentioned and the next board ended up having to pay Gregory compensation.

BEWARE THE LETTER B

Commencing with the 1999/2000 season, the Rams went through a bizarre run of fortune in the FA Cup draw. Each season they found themselves drawn against a lower division team whose name began with the letter B. The four in question were; Burnley, Blackburn Rovers, Bristol Rovers and Brentford. Despite, on the first three occasions, having home advantage at some stage of the tie, they lost each game. Most embarrassing was a 3-1 reverse against basement-division side Bristol Rovers. The club would have been delighted to get drawn against Ipswich Town at the end of the cycle. Sadly they managed to lose that one as well.

TOO MANY RAMS

When the Rams were relegated from the Premiership at the end of 2001/02, they had used a record high number of players in an attempt to survive. A total of 34 stepped out over the white line – two more than the previous high.

THE SETH SALE

In the relegation season of 2001/02, Derby County still managed to break their own record for the transfer fee of an outgoing player. Seth Johnson, who had been a fans' favourite in his time at Pride Park, moved to Leeds United for a phenomenal £7m – it is a figure that still stands to this day.

THE THREE AMIGOS

There have been numerous directors, and a number of different owners, in the history of Derby County, but none stirred up as much controversy as the Jeremy Keith-led consortium that purchased the club for £3 in 2003. The gang of three had no connections with the area, and bought the club cheaply after ensuring it had been placed into receivership long enough to negate all shares belonging to stockholders. After several years of control, Derby County was purchased by a group of local businessmen and Keith and several of his colleagues were charged with financial illegalities and jailed.

RAMS ON THE SLIDE

Demotion from the Premier League in 2001/02 nearly became a real disaster as the Rams failed to halt the slide and ended their first campaign back in the second tier a mere six points off the drop zone. Lack of consistency was clearly a problem, and the club broke their own record for number of players used – a whopping 36.

BURLEY A BIG HIT

George Burley was initially brought to the club to fill the void left by the suspension of John Gregory. He did such a good job that he turned the club from relegation candidates to play-off contenders almost overnight. The Rams went from 20th place at the end of 2003/04 to fourth at the end of 2004/05.

LEWIN A RISING STAR

When Lewin Nyatanga made his Wales Under-21 debut he joined a select group of players who represented their country before making first-team debuts for their clubs. For Nyatanga it was not only a proud moment but it also propelled him into the record books. He was only 16 years and 174 days old when he made his international debut in 2004 – a Wales record at that point.

THE DERBY COUNTY TRAWLER

One of the strangest honours bestowed on the football club was having a fishing trawler named in its honour. The boat, which was named *Derby County*, was built in Middlesbrough and took to sea in September 1933. It served the war effort as an anti-submarine vessel, and was returned to fishing duties after the war. It was scrapped in 1964.

AN ACRIMONIOUS DEPARTURE

George Burley did a tremendous job as manager in trying circumstances. He took the club from the relegation zone to fourth place, and even if the play-offs proved an anti-climax the team seemed to be heading in the right direction. Burley quit during the summer, however, claiming that director of football Murdo Mackay was interfering with his managerial duties.

HOT ON THE DRAW

The Rams only lost 16 of their 46 matches in the 2005/06 season. Their problem was converting draws into victories. They tied a record-breaking 20 league games. The 50 points they gained meant that they finished the season just eight above the drop zone. Converting ten of the 20 draws would have seen them finish seventh.

TRUST IN THE FANS

Supporters have always been the lifeblood of Derby County but never more so than during the dying days of the Jeremy Keith regime. A supporters' trust of concerned fans was an important part of the efforts to ask questions and force out the board. They eventually got their wish when a group of local businessmen headed by former director and vice chairman Peter Gadsby brought the club back into local ownership. The new consortium was given a rapturous pitchside welcome on their unveiling.

LEWIN NYATANGA MADE HIS WALES UNDER-21 DEBUT BEFORE HE MADE A SENIOR APPEARANCE FOR THE RAMS

TOP TEN APPEARANCES – 2. RON WEBSTER

'Unflappable', 'loyal', 'consistent' and with 'no lack of ability' are just a few things that have been said about Ron Webster. Born in Belper, Ron is the one local link to both of the championship-winning sides in the 1970s. But his association with the club started well before, and finished long after, those glory days. He first served the club as a young right-back under Harry Storer, who left the Baseball Ground in 1962, which shows just how long Ron had been a part of the set-up. Ron showed plenty of promise in those early days and really started to establish himself in the team under Tim Ward with Derby plodding along in the Second Division and showing no signs of going anywhere. The arrival of Brian Clough and Peter Taylor changed all of that in 1967 and they appreciated the value that Ron gave them. Bigger clubs had become aware of Ron but he remained loyal to Derby and was rewarded with a career that saw him go through the real highs that the club was soon to encounter. As a player, he largely went under the radar, not helped by performing in one of the game's more unglamorous positions, but he was a regular in the team as Derby rose from the middle-reaches of the Second Division to the top of the English game, and he was certainly appreciated by all those who worked with him. He wasn't one to make the most of the limelight, preferring instead to quietly go about his business with the minimum of fuss – but with the maximum of effectiveness.

But on rare occasions he would pop up in unexpected style to score a goal, notching one in each of the title-winning seasons in an overall tally that didn't get out of single figures despite him playing 535 games for the club. For a time, Ron had made more appearances in a Derby County shirt than any other and it wasn't until Kevin Hector returned to the Baseball Ground that his record was overhauled. Ron won the Player of the Year award in the turbulent 1973/74 season and even when Rod Thomas arrived for the following campaign, he was still a fixture in the side until losing his place because of injury. Ron retired after his last game as a player in 1977 but continued to serve the club as a respected and effective youth coach until losing his role in the early 1980s. In 2009 he was voted the greatest right-back in the history of Derby County Football Club.

TWO TEAMS TO DEBUT

The inability to field a settled side has always been a recipe for disaster. The 2005/06 season was no different. Not only did the Rams get through a staggering 39 different players during the campaign, no fewer than 22 of them were debutants.

THE SMALL GIANT

Steve Bloomer was undoubtedly a giant of the game; it was a different matter on the pitch though. The most prolific goalscorer in Rams history stood a mere 5ft 7ins. tall in his bare feet.

BILLY FLIES IN

When Billy Davies was unveiled as the new Rams manager in 2006, his introduction to the media was different to anything that had gone before. Jill Marples, who along with her husband at the time, Peter – part of the consortium of local business people running the club – was a licence-holding helicopter pilot. Thus it was that Davies descended from the heavens on to the training pitches at Moor Farm to meet the press.

CHEAP AT TWICE THE PRICE

Steve Bloomer was considered such an important player for the Rams, the club were prepared to pay him way in excess of any of the other members of the squad for his services – his team-mates only picked up £3 a week while Bloomer took home a staggering £5.

A PROGRAMME FOR SIX PENCE

The matchday programme for the 1946 FA Cup final had a cover price of sixpence (2.5p). There are still a number of copies around these days but £200 is not an unknown price for such an item.

TURNING OUT FOR TED

An all-star line-up of ex-professionals turned out on behalf of ex-Rams winger Ted McMinn on May 1st 2006. A game was arranged between former Derby County and Rangers players, plus a few other footballing personalities. The game provided supporters with the bizarre sight of Stuart Pearce kissing the Rams badge on his shirt after scoring for the Derby County side.

BROWN ON THE HUNT

When Phil Brown took over as manager it was on the understanding that although he had never bossed a team before, he had many of the necessary skills to do so. The directors would provide him with all the support needed to do the job. Sadly, the help did not stretch to providing him with an experienced assistant. The owners argued that Phil had overspent on players and would, therefore, have to shop at the lower end of the market for a number two. Brown was forced to hire Dean Holdsworth who (though subsequently going on to prove himself an able manager) had no more experience at the time as an assistant, than his boss had as a manager.

BILLY MAKES IT THREE

The brief given to Billy Davies when he took up the Pride Park reins was to put together a three-year plan to return the Derby County to the top flight. It worked better than even Davies could have imagined as the club were propelled into the Premiership at the end of his first season in charge via the play-offs. Davies is one of only three managers to achieve such a feat.

BEN'S TRAGIC TIME

One of the most tragic players for the Rams before World War I was Ben Warren. He played 242 times for Derby before their relegation. He moved to Chelsea where he suffered a mental breakdown while out with a long-term injury. He died of tuberculosis in 1917 at the Derbyshire Lunatic Asylum.

COOPER'S LEGACY

One good thing came out of the tragic death of ex-Rams player Tommy Cooper, who died in a motorcycle accident in World War II. As a result of his death the wearing of motorcycle helmets by dispatch riders became compulsory.

TON A TICKET

A ticket for the Rams' 1946 FA Cup final victory over Charlton Athletic could be purchased for three shillings and sixpence (17.5 pence). According to noted Derby County memorabilia expert Andy Ellis a used stub for that game would now be worth up to £100.

TEN GREAT HOME MATCHES DERBY 3 LIVERPOOL 2

If the Rams had made progress in their second season in the Premier League, their third saw them seriously threaten qualification for the Uefa Cup. By the onset of spring they were serious contenders to reach Europe, either via the Premiership or the FA Cup. The latter route had been snuffed out a week prior to this fixture after a last-minute defeat at Arsenal in the quarter-final. In the league they were sitting behind Aston Villa, who they then beat 2-1 in midweek, and Liverpool, who were vanquished in front of what was at the time a Pride Park record attendance of 32,913. The fans inside the stadium on that sunny March afternoon were given a real treat as not only did Jim Smith's side collect three points, they did so with a brand of football that was easy on the eye and up there with the best they had played all season. Only 12 minutes were on the clock when Deon Burton rose to open the scoring, nodding home a Lars Bohinen corner, but a visiting forward line of Robbie Fowler and Michael Owen was always going to cause problems. The Reds equalised when Fowler smashed home a penalty after Owen had been felled but Derby were back in front by half-time, again with a header, as Paulo Wanchope met Igor Stimac's inviting free kick to find the corner past David James. The second half was only five minutes old when the same combination led to the Rams going 3-1 ahead. Liverpool were sleeping when Stimac lofted a quick free kick forward and Wanchope escaped his marker, took it down and hammered his shot into the net. Bohinen then produced one of Pride Park's greatest-ever misses as he failed from nothing more than a few yards with the ball at his feet. Dominic Matteo made the clearance and soon set up Fowler for his second to create an air of tension around the stadium as Derby found themselves under real pressure.

But, what they faced, they dealt with well, and they might have added to their tally. In the end, they got their reward for an outstanding afternoon. Derby's form tailed away in the last few weeks of the season and they missed out on Europe but still finished eighth, their best since coming fifth under Arthur Cox in 1988/89. Only four teams left Pride Park with all three points during 1998/99, so strong was their home record.

WELL DONE YOUNG JIM

At the age of 22, Jim Bullions was the youngest Derby County player to feature in the FA Cup final. One of just 11 players to earn FA Cup winners' medals with the Rams, he only played 29 times for the club in total – with 12 of those being FA Cup ties.

A REAL RECORD

The record attendance for a competitive fixture involving Derby County is a staggering 120,000. The match in question was the European Cup second-round second leg away to Real Madrid. The Rams held a 4-1 advantage from the Baseball Ground first leg, but went out of the competition by virtue of losing 5-1 in Spain.

BERT MAKES AMENDS

The first post-war FA Cup final was certainly not without incident, but would probably have reached full time goalless if not for the efforts of Charlton full-back Bert Turner. It was Turner who deflected the ball into his own net to give the Rams the lead, and Turner whose free kick brought the two sides back level.

A TRUE STOREY

March 1972 provided Derby County fans with the player that never was. Ian Storey-Moore was the star player of local rivals Nottingham Forest at the time of Brian Clough's attempts to add him to the Rams squad. Terry Hennessey and Alan Hinton had already made similar moves, much to the chagrin of those running Forest. Storey-Moore was paraded in front of the Derby fans before all the paperwork had been completed. Forest had second thoughts and sold the player to Manchester United leaving all at Derby wondering what might have been.

BANG WENT THE BALL

If it had not been for shoddy workmanship, the Rams would probably have won the 1946 FA Cup final in normal time. Taking aim for what would have been the match-winning goal, Jack Stamps could only watch the ball burst as he was about to let fly. A replacement ball was introduced to the game, but the moment had gone and a scoreline of 1-1 at full time meant extra time.

HECTOR GOAL A FIRST

Disappointing though losing the first leg semi-final against Juventus was, it did provide the Rams with one impressive 'first'. Kevin Hector's goal in the game was the first scored by an English team in Italy in a European Cup tie since the competition began in 1955.

ON THE RIGHT TRACK

If someone had suggested that *Derby County* was on the right track between 1936 and 1959 they could have been talking about the football club, but were more likely discussing the passenger locomotive named in the club's honour that ran up and down the East Coast.

BOARD CAVE IN

The Rams were deserved winners of the 1946 FA Cup final, but it was nearly a walkover for opponents Charlton Athletic. With only a few days until the game, Derby players threatened to withdraw their services unless the uncovered seats provided for loved ones were upgraded to the covered ones provided for the wives of directors. Unsurprisingly, the board acceded to the demands.

FIVE-A-SIDE STARS

One of the less well-known successes of the Rams in their 1970s heyday was victory in the *Daily Express* five-a-side tournament. The tournament, which was held at the Wembley Arena, featured teams comprising of players from the biggest clubs in the land. Sandwiched between the two First Division titles, they picked up the trophy in 1973.

PITCHING FEAR

The Baseball Ground pitch had been the subject of much controversy for a long while. Once the winter arrived it rapidly became more a mud heap than a grassy playing surface. The decision was taken to rip it up and replace it with a brand new one at the end of the 1974/75 season. Fans wondered if the change would make a difference, and initially had every reason to be concerned as the first competitive fixture played on it saw Queens Park Rangers romp to a 5-1 victory. Normal order was soon restored though as the Rams ended the season in fourth place.

A GAME OF THREE HALVES

The Rams once actually played a game of three halves. The match was at Sunderland on September 1st 1894. The appointed referee, a certain Mr Kirkham, failed to arrive in time for kick-off, but the match started as scheduled with a stand-in official. When Kirkham arrived at half-time he decided that the 45 minutes played were null and void, and the match recommenced with the 3-0 scoreline in favour of the hosts ruled out. It made no difference as Derby proceeded to lose the next 90 minutes 8-0. The 135-minute game is the longest in club history.

WATER WELCOME

Qualifying for European football brought some of the big names of the game to Derby for the first time, and although the citizens of Derbyshire knew all about the likes of Benfica and Eusebio, it is fair to say that the reverse was not true. To give the Portuguese side a welcome they would not forget for the game on October 25th 1972, the Baseball Ground pitch was heavily watered ahead of the game. When the opposition visited the stadium it is said that they had seen nothing like the playing surface ever before, and were beaten when they saw the mud oozing above their designer shoes, long before the game even kicked off.

BOB ON THE SPOT

On April 30th 1977, Bob Smith became an unlikely television star. Smith was groundsman at the Baseball Ground when Manchester City came to visit. With two minutes remaining, the referee awarded the Rams a penalty, only to look in horror as he pointed to where the penalty spot should have been. The goalmouth had been churned up during the game to the extent that the markings had disappeared. The groundsman was summoned to repaint the penalty spot. Smith measured out the distance from the goal-line and painted a new white spot from where Gerry Daly netted the fourth and final goal of the afternoon.

OVER ALLOCATED

It is certainly true that the Rams' appearance in the first post-war FA Cup final attracted the public imagination. The club was issued an allocation of 12,000 tickets, but received approximately 1,000,000 applications.

NOT ALL GAMES LAST 90 MINUTES

The Rams found themselves the subject of controversy on April 14th 1983 by forcing the referee to end a game 78 seconds short. The final match of the season at home to Fulham had the potential to relegate the hosts and promote the visitors. Fans were allowed to spill onto the Baseball Ground during the closing stages of the match which Derby were winning 1-0. When the referee blew for offside fans misinterpreted the signal as the end of the game and invaded the pitch to celebrate. The referee took both teams off and refused to restart the match. The only time a league game has been allowed to end early.

RAMS' LAST LAUGH

Derby County and Leeds United were bitter rivals in the 1970s but Rams fans had the last laugh at the end of the 1969/70 campaign thanks to an error of judgement by Leeds manager Don Revie. With European and FA Cup glory beckoning the Yorkshire outfit, Revie named a reserve side to travel to the Baseball Ground on March 30th 1970. His team were beaten 4-1, the club then fined for deliberately naming a weakened side, and Leeds went on to lose both the FA Cup final and both legs of the European Cup semi-final.

SCORING IN SECONDS

While Kevin Hector features in the fastest goal ever scored for his exploits before joining the Rams, Derby County themselves played their part in one of the three quickest goals ever scored. Unfortunately, they were on the receiving end. Crystal Palace were the visitors to the Baseball Ground on December 12th 1964 and it was Keith Smith who applied the final touch to a strike that was officially timed at six seconds.

JACK DEFIES HITLER

Rams fans may discover, to their horror, photographs of their team giving the Nazi salute. The players were not sympathisers of the regime but merely following instructions from the British Foreign Office. Derby had been invited to play several exhibition matches in Germany, and the Foreign Office had told them to make the salute for fears of insulting Hitler and causing an international incident. All the players followed the instruction apart from goalkeeper Jack Kirby.

EARLY ACTION ON CAMERA

A between wars Derby County were caught on film on January 26th 1935. Swansea Town were visitors for an FA Cup fourth-round tie. News cameras filmed Derby on fine form as they beat the Swans 3-0.

THE COFFEE CUP GOAL

One of the most bizarre goal assists in the history of the game came during a Pride Park match against local rivals Nottingham Forest. The date was March 20th 2004 and the assist was from a plastic coffee cup that had blown onto the field of play. It gained its place in club history when the ball deflected off it via Forest goalkeeper Barry Roche's mis-hit clearance to Paul Peschisolido, who duly scored.

A STATUE OF JIMMY

Steve Bloomer is not the only Derby County player to be honoured by a sculpture. Jimmy Hagan, who was one of the Sheffield United all-time greats, started his professional career with the Rams. He played 30 games for the Baseball Ground outfit before being sold to the South Yorkshire club. His statue was unveiled at Bramall Lane in 2001.

STARS ON TV

The first televised appearance by the Rams in a football match occurred on November 17th 1956. The programme was *Sports Special* and the match in question was an FA Cup first-round home tie against Bradford City. Derby celebrated with a 2-1 victory.

RAMS GO LIVE

November 22nd 1987 went down in history as a great day for armchair followers of Derby County, for this was the first live league game featuring the Rams. Arthur Cox's men were pitted against Chelsea and emerged winners by a scoreline of 2-0. Steve Cross and John Gregory were the scorers.

BBG A SCREEN STAR

The Baseball Ground itself enjoyed a spell as a television star. The stadium was used to represent the home ground of Third Division Dunmore United in a television series entitled *Murphy's Mob*.

TOP TEN APPEARANCES – 1. KEVIN HECTOR

It is entirely appropriate that a man known fondly among Derby supporters as 'The King' has made more appearances for Derby County than any other player. A fee of £38,000 in 1966 saw him come to the Baseball Ground, one of Tim Ward's great acts, although eyes were certainly opened by a run-of-the-mill Second Division side splashing that sort of cash. However, Kevin had already scored more than a century of Football League goals for Bradford Park Avenue and if ever there was a case of speculating to accumulate paying off, this was it. Kevin was a pre-Brian Clough member of the Baseball Ground set-up but was integral to the successes over the coming years. He was a promotion-winner in 1969 and following promotion to the top flight, between 1970 and 1972, he played in 105 consecutive games. In fact, such was his durability, from August 1967 to December 1974 he missed just four of a possible 314 league fixtures, a remarkable achievement for a striker. For a man with such grace and class it is a mystery how he won only two England caps – both as a substitute in 1973 – particularly as he was the Rams' Player of the Year in 1972/73 and barely missed a match in the two title-winning campaigns.

He helped Derby to the semi-final of the European Cup in 1973 where his goal away at Juventus in the first leg was the first conceded by any Italian side on home soil to English opposition in the competition's history. Although he scored 201 goals over his two spells, a figure beaten only by Steve Bloomer, Kevin was more than just a goalscorer – he was a linker of play, a provider too, great on the ball and with wonderful awareness of the game around him. Tommy Docherty let him leave the Baseball Ground, for Canadian side Vancouver Whitecaps, but after two years Kevin returned to Derby like the prodigal son coming home. Goals were less regular in his second spell, due largely to often playing in a deeper midfield role, but bowing out with his 201st and final goal in his 589th and final game on the last day of the 1981/82 season was a perfect way to end a great career with the club. Kevin has continued to pull on a Derby County shirt into his 60s in charity and fundraising matches, and even scored his first overhead kick at the age of 59!

THE INJURY THIRD

The most injury time added on to a game involving Derby County was a staggering 14 minutes – added to the end of the first half in a match at Grimsby Town on August 17th 2002. Danny Higginbotham of Derby and Grimsby's Steve Livingstone clashed heads, and with the Mariners striker clearly in a bad way it took some considerable time for treatment to be carried out on the pitch to Livingstone before the player was taken to hospital. Thankfully, he later made a full recovery.

QUESTIONING THE LIGHTS

One unpleasant aftermath of the Derby County versus Wimbledon abandonment because of floodlight failure was a suggestion that the match had been the subject of evil intent by a Far East gambling consortium. Conspiracy theorists had noticed that this was one of four games that had suffered similar problems in a short space of time. All involved London clubs, with Wimbledon affected in a match against Arsenal. Investigations proved that three of the games had been abandoned after tampering with the lights. Derby's problem, however, was not one of them and the problem in their case was found to be an overloaded fuse.

LEE V HUNTER

The most famous sending off in Rams history took place on November 1st 1975. Leeds were visitors to the Baseball Ground, and an ongoing battle between Francis Lee and Norman Hunter led to fisticuffs in the penalty area and the sending off of both players. Matters became worse as a further round of punches were thrown by the combatants as they left the pitch, and a free-for-all briefly ensued as players from both teams weighed in. Derby had the last laugh on the day, emerging victorious 3-2.

AN OLD MASCOT

For many young Derby County fans, the chance to lead the team out as matchday mascots has been a memory to treasure. Some mascots are in their teens, but the majority are youngsters still at junior school. The oldest recorded mascot was 35 years of age. Going by the name of Simon Groom, he was actually a *Blue Peter* presenter, as well as a lifelong fan of the club, and he was given the honour of leading the team out while making a feature for the television show about the Rams. However, it is not known whether he presented the squad with *Blue Peter* badges.

TEN GREAT HOME MATCHES DERBY 3 FOREST 0

The list of Pride Park wins over Nottingham Forest has plenty of options but for a 90-minute display of football that completely outclassed the visitors from along the A52, you have to go a long way to beat this one. George Burley's teams have always had reputations as ones to play the ball around well and in his second season at Derby, the Scot was making his impact felt. The Rams were coming together nicely thanks to some shrewd acquisitions the previous summer and started this match as favourites against the struggling Reds.

It didn't take them long to show just why that was with a remarkable flowing move that started with Ian Taylor and involved Jeff Kenna, Morten Bisgaard and Inigo Idiakez before Tommy Smith applied the finishing touch to send the home fans into raptures. Another crowd of more than 30,000 was inside the stadium with the vast majority looking for the home side to repeat their efforts of the previous season's dramatic 4-2 success, remembered mainly for the assist from a coffee cup. Forest tried for a swift response but Derby found themselves with a great chance to make it 2-0 with only 20 minutes gone as they were awarded a penalty – but skipper Taylor blazed his shot over the bar and into the massed ranks of visiting fans behind the goal.

The Reds certainly weren't going to go down without a fight and they made life difficult at times for Burley's men, although they rarely gave a serious threat of an equaliser. But, without a second goal to cheer, the home fans weren't truly able to relax, although any nerves were lifted in the 75th minute. Smith turned provider with a deep cross to the far post that Polish striker Grzegorz Rasiak got on the end of with a powerful header to make it 2-0. Derby were able to enjoy themselves for the final 15 minutes and when they added a third, there was another touch of class to the move. The ball broke to Taylor, who pinged a first-time pass out to Bisgaard on the right. Bisgaard didn't take a touch either, side-footing in a lovely low ball that got a suitable finishing touch from Rasiak. This was the first match between Derby and Forest since the death of Brian Clough, and both sets of fans paid glowing tributes to the man who had been such a legend with both clubs.

WOLFIE'S RAMS SCARF

Robert Lindsay is renowned as a lifelong Derby County supporter, and is known to current Rams fans not only for his many television appearances but as lead singer on the Derby anthem Steve Bloomer's Watching You. Relatively few fans would know that he publicly showed his allegiances as far back as the *Citizen Smith* comedy show in the late 1970s. Playing a character that supposedly supported Fulham, Lindsay regularly ensured that the black and white football scarf he was wearing was not a Fulham one but his Rams scarf.

LIVE FROM ITALY

The Rams had to wait until 1973 for their first full live match on television. The game in question was the European Cup semi-final first leg against Juventus. BBC broadcast the tie which would have disappointed most of those watching as it ended 3-1 in favour of the Italians.

LIKE FRED KARNO'S ARMY

Supporters of a certain age would describe poor playing performances by the Rams as being like Fred Karno's Army – in reference to a famous music hall comedy act. One-time Derby County full-back Jack Kifford would have more idea than most of the truth of such a statement. He only played six times for the club before moving on, but after his career was over he actually became part of Karno's troupe where he performed alongside Charlie Chaplin and Stan Laurel.

CENTURY-OLD FILM

The oldest known film footage of Derby County in action – and the only clips of Steve Bloomer as a player – dates right back to March 13th 1911, and an FA Cup tie at Newcastle. It was an inauspicious screen debut for the Rams who fell to a miserable 4-0 defeat.

MATCH OF THE DAY

The first appearance by the Rams on *Match of the Day* was towards the end of the television show's first season. The date was April 10th 1965 and Derby County were playing away at Northampton Town. Viewers were treated to four goals in all as the match ended 2-2. Alan Durban was responsible for both Derby goals.

KEEPER AND THE KING

If any Derby County footballer can have been touched by greatness it would have to be goalkeeper Ian Feuer, who enjoyed a short loan spell at the club at the turn of the 21st century. A keeper with a more than respectable record, he was famous more for his associations than his ability in his time at Derby as his sister was a film actress who had been married to Mickey Rourke at one stage, and his father was a musician who had backed both Frank Sinatra and Elvis Presley.

JOHN'S CURLING GLORY

Many footballers have shown what fine all-round athletes they are by excelling at other sports. John Goodall, though, is the only Derby County footballer to date to become England champion of the Scottish sport of curling.

SIX PAST MORRIS

Charlie Morris is the holder of a unique place in Rams history. A full-back by trade, Morris played his part in the worst FA Cup final result of all time – the 1903, 6-0 defeat to Bury – in goal because of injury to the regular keeper. Unperturbed by the experience, Morris had a spell between the sticks for Wales during a 7-1 defeat at home to England.

A PAINFUL TACKLE

Mart Poom is, as far as anyone can be certain, the only player in Derby County history to be injured by a heavy metal band while playing football. The Estonian, while on holiday in his home town of Tallinn, accepted the offer to play in a charity match against rock band Iron Maiden, who were touring. Deciding to play as a striker, Poom was caught by a wild tackle and picked up an injury that may tactfully be described as damaging his chances of increasing the size of his family. Rams boss Jim Smith did not know whether to laugh or cry when told of the injury to his player.

BETWEEN THE POSTS

Three times during Derby County history, Rams outfield players have been forced to play entire matches between the posts because of extraordinary circumstances. The trio comprises Jack Nicholas, John Goodall, and Arthur Latham.

THREE STOPPERS

March 10th 2010 goes down in history as the first (and so far only) occasion in Rams history that they have fielded three different goalkeepers in one match – away at Reading. Problems began in the 13th minute when first-choice keeper Steven Bywater injured his back. Derby had a substitute keeper available in Saul Deeney and the Irishman took up his place between the posts. Deeney lasted until the 41st minute when he was dismissed for a foul in the penalty area. Captain Robbie Savage took over for the rest of the game, and only did marginally worse than the two proper keepers by conceding two goals as opposed to their one apiece.

SUTTON'S STRANGE END

One of the most mysterious substitutions in club history came at Bramall Lane on October 7th 1995. Despite not being beaten, goalkeeper Steve Sutton, who was not injured, was replaced during the half-time interval by Russell Hoult. Sutton played 95 games for the Rams in two spells at the club, but never featured again for the first team.

SHORT SHRIFT FOR LES

Les Green was another keeper to be summarily consigned to the margins. Not the tallest of shot stoppers, he was considered a player of tremendous consistency. He made 129 consecutive appearances for the club, but was dropped after conceding four goals at home to Manchester United on December 26th 1970. It was his last game for the first team.

POOM'S TOWERING HEADER

Mart Poom experienced the most unusual hero's return for a visiting ex-player when coming back to Pride Park. The Estonian shot stopper was arguably the best goalkeeper that the Rams have had since the departure of Peter Shilton. Poom moved on to play for Sunderland, and was greeted with a warm and friendly welcome by Derby fans on his first return to the club as an opposing player. The hosts took the lead through Ian Taylor, as the game entered stoppage time, and as a last throw of the dice the Estonian went up for a Sunderland corner deep in stoppage time. Incredibly, Poom got his head to the incoming corner and scored an unlikely equaliser.

RAMS ON COURT

There would be many complaints these days if anyone tried to play a game of football on the beautifully manicured courts of the Queen's Club in Kensington. Now known as a top venue for tennis, 11 Derby County players did just that on April 17th 1897. The Rams were there to fulfil a fixture against Corinthians. The match ended 4-4.

OLYMPIC HEROES

Three footballers who have represented Derby County can boast of being Olympic gold medallists at the sport. The team they represented was actually named United Kingdom and the trio of winners were Herbert Smith and Horace Bailey in the 1908 London Olympics and Ivan Sharpe four years later in Stockholm.

J P JOHN'S FOREST TREBLE

John Barrington Trapnell Chevalier was the son of a preacher man who deserves mention in any book to be read by Rams fans. His CV makes impressive reading; he was a Justice of the Peace, and he had already played in four FA Cup finals by the time he reached Derby County. His place in club legends is assured, though, because he scored the first hat-trick against local rivals Nottingham Forest. The match, a friendly, was the first meeting between the two sides and ended in a 6-1 victory for the visiting Derby side.

STORER'S DUAL ROLE

Derby County manager Harry Storer was renowned as a sporting all-rounder, and proved just how adept he was at sports other than football by turning out nine times for Derbyshire County Cricket Club in their only County Championship-winning season of 1936, while also employed as manager at Coventry City.

BRIAN TAKES ACTION

Brian McCord only made ten appearances in a Derby shirt, including three as a substitute, before moving on to Stockport County. His career was ended by a tackle from Swansea player John Cornforth. He rates a mention here, though, because he successfully sued for damages through the High Court. The £50,000 interim award was the first such action by a footballer to reach a successful conclusion.

THE TIN MAN

There is virtually no player in the modern game not to have a nickname; some are provided by team-mates, and some courtesy of the supporters. Very few have a more unusual one than Ted McMinn who was christened 'The Tin Man'. The name came about because it was felt that his unusual running style was reminiscent of one of the characters in *The Wizard of Oz*.

TAH PEI GAN RAMS

There are probably not many Rams fans who would admit to supporting a club named Tah Pei Gan, but in truth every single one of them do precisely that. The bizarre change dates back to the 1990s when bookmakers in China noticed the problems that some of their customers had when requesting Derby County. As a result they utilised various Chinese syllables to make a local approximation of the sounds of the original.

DOUGLAS TO DALLY

Dally Duncan is another player whose nickname caused considerable confusion. It turned out that the epithet had its origins in his childhood habit of dawdling along behind his father when out. His persistent habit of dallying behind led to the unusual nickname.

DOC AT THE WORLD CUP

The first individual with a Derby County connection to take part in a World Cup finals was Tommy Docherty. Admittedly, the year was 1954, nearly a quarter of a century before he arrived at the Baseball Ground as manager, but he enjoyed almost as much success in his national team's contribution to the tournament as his own personal part in the Derby County story – the Scots lost both their matches without scoring a solitary goal.

BLOOMER'S LAST GOAL

He may have ended his league career shortly before the outbreak of World War I, but it was long after the return to peace that he kicked his last ball. At the age of 57, Bloomer entertained the crowd for the final time as the captain of Belper British Legion in a charity match. His side lost the match but the striker went out on a high by scoring a penalty.

A BROTHERLY APPOINTMENT

When Billy Davies introduced a number of additional backroom staff to prepare the club at all levels for the adventure that was to be the first season back in the Premier League, no-one paid much attention to the new reserve-team manager, even though Davies sang the praises of a man who had been a vital source of information from North America while working over there. The Derby boss also failed to mention that it was not mere coincidence that the man in charge of the second string had the same surname as him. Reserve-team manager John Davies was in fact the manager's brother.

SIBLING SIGNING

Although there have been many instances of fathers and sons – or pairs of brothers – both playing for Derby County, the reasoning has usually been because it is believed, or at least assumed, that both have inherited a share of the talent. That was definitely not the case for Harry Atkin. It was brother Jack that the Rams were interested in. Jack Atkin insisted that if they sign him then they had to sign his brother too. Harry was not considered good enough, but the club still signed him and split the wage they were intending giving to brother Jack between the pair of them.

FOR JUST THREE PENCE A WEEK

Alick Grant showed that he had the necessary intelligence to be a teacher (his chosen profession) when negotiating his salary with Derby County in 1946. Unlike some, he did not request large amounts of money. He knew that he would only continue to be eligible for family allowance while doing his teacher training if the club paid him less than a certain amount. As a result, he drew a mere three pence a week from the Rams.

A MARATHON OF HEATING

When Derby County relocated to Pride Park the board of directors were keen to ensure that there was minimum chance of games being postponed because of bad weather. To that end, they had a staggering 26 miles of undersoil heating installed beneath the playing surface. So far the policy seems to have worked as no game has yet been called off because of a frozen surface.

GREGORY'S UNHAPPY RETURN

John Gregory was one of a number of Derby County players who went on to manage the club. As with so many things, timing is crucial, and while as a player he was brought in at the right moment to lead Arthur Cox's side to double promotions when he arrived at a club on the slide. With neither Jim Smith nor Colin Todd able to arrest the decline, in the 2001/02 season the board looked to the man who had turned around Aston Villa's fortunes. The Rams flickered back into winning ways briefly but could not sustain the improvement and Derby County went down. In their reduced circumstances, the club carried an unsustainable wage bill and Gregory set about adjusting it. He told some of the Rams' big earners that they were no longer required and to look for new clubs during the close season. Still under contract, they all reported back for pre-season training, but with relations between manager and some of his squad decidedly frosty. With none of his wage bill cut, there was little opportunity for team rebuilding, although he did retain the experienced pairing of Rob Lee and Warren Barton, who he brought in to aid the ultimately unsuccessful battle for Premier League survival. Even with the lack of investment and apparent discord in the camp, the Rams got off to a decent start with two wins in their first three matches but inconsistency remained a problem, shown by the fact that they only earned back-to-back wins on two occasions while Gregory remained at the helm. Twice they managed unbeaten runs of four games but even during those spells they found it very difficult to finish off opponents and only picked up 14 points out of 24. When they won, however, they were capable of winning well. Gregory was keen to give youth its head and provided Izale McLeod with a first-team debut before he had ever turned out for the reserves, and made Lee Holmes the youngest player in Derby history with a substitute appearance against Grimsby. With the scent of history in his nostrils, he brought the same player on as a substitute in the FA Cup at Brentford, thus making him the youngest player in the FA Cup proper at that stage. The latter stages of the season seemed to be drifting to an uninspiring conclusion when the board suddenly announced they were suspending Gregory pending an investigation. No reason was given and Gregory collected compensation from a later board.

THE SECOND CLOUGH COMING

The arrival of Nigel Clough as manager at Pride Park brought excitement, but also expectation. His record at Burton had established his credentials as a man who knew what he was doing as the Brewers rose from non-league obscurity to the verge of League Two. If that was not enough, he had the family name to add a little extra spice. Given his ability to work to a very tight budget it quickly became apparent that it would be his fiscal prudence to the fore rather than his father's reputation. Clough's brief was to slash the wage bill, reduce the size of the squad, and keep the club away from the murky waters of the relegation zone. The first game after his appointment was announced was against Manchester United at Pride Park in the League Cup. Derby won 1-0 and although that was the high-point of his first term in charge, the side finished eight points above the drop zone. Nigel's masterstroke was to reintroduce Robbie Savage to the team after the player had been marginalised by Paul Jewell. Savage proved inspirational as on-field leader, both for his captaincy and his passing ability. The summer provided Clough with the opportunity to bring in new players. Shaun Barker was the big money move and the centre-half, despite struggling for fitness, proved a valuable capture. Less impressive was the introduction of Lee Croft from Norwich. Arguably the most important arrival at that time, though, was Johnny Metgod as coach. There were highs in the first full season for the new boss, with a 5-3 win over Preston North End and a run in the FA Cup. There were also lows, most spectacularly losing 6-1 at Cardiff. The overall picture showed an improvement in position and points total from the previous campaign. More signings during summer 2010 saw the arrival of both John Brayford and James Bailey from Crewe, a double purchase that proved that Nigel Clough could spot lower league talent as well as anyone. There were also less successful arrivals such as David Martin. A run of games from October to November had the Rams playing the best football in the division and, for a brief spell, supporters found themselves talking excitedly about promotion. The wheels started to come off after taking a one-goal lead at Burnley only to lose 2-1, and the rest of the season was spent keeping heads just above water. Derby never dropped into the bottom three. A big summer loomed for Clough who knew he had to get things right this time.

BOB'S LAST ACT

Many players throughout football history have committed fouls which they have later regretted as their actions may have cost them and team-mates the game. Not many, however, have made a mistake so disastrous as to cost them their club career. Bob Saxton would have to admit to doing precisely that. The central defender conceded a stupid and needless handball in his own penalty area during the League Cup semi-final first leg at the Baseball Ground against Leeds United in 1968. The ensuing spot kick was all that separated the two sides at the end of the game. For Brian Clough it was all too much and Saxton never pulled on a Derby County shirt again.

GROUNDSTAFF'S BIG EFFORT

There is a lot of talk about the amount of ground covered by players and referees during the course of a 90-minute game, but supporters should, perhaps, spare a thought for the poor groundsman. It has been estimated that cutting the grass both length and width ways, and then adding all the white lines and markings, makes for a total distance of 19 miles.

EXORCISING THE SPIRIT

According to Rams legend, a longstanding gypsy curse, dating back to the club's move to the Baseball Ground, had ensured bad luck forevermore, or at least until a bunch of gypsies were paid off ahead of the 1946 FA Cup final. After the acrimonious departure of Brian Clough and Peter Taylor, someone had the bright idea that the curse had either returned or not been lifted properly. This time a local psychic named Doreen Shadbolt was brought in to investigate. She claimed that there was a spirit in one of the Baseball Ground penalty areas and arranged an exorcism. It is difficult to say whether the results were successful or not as the fortunes of Derby County have remained as variable as they ever were.

PEM HAUNTS HATTERS

Whether it was sour grapes or economics, Mark Pembridge had an excellent day ruined when he returned to his old club Luton Town and scored a hat-trick. His former employers broke with tradition and refused to let him take the match ball back home.

A SUPERNATURAL DEFEAT

Doreen Shadbolt is not the only female with mystic powers to be summoned to the Baseball Ground in an attempt to ward off evil spirits and lift curses; there are also the supernatural powers of Aveline Lee to celebrate. Lee conducted her own form of exorcism in front of television cameras in 1993. Her ceremony consisted of mystical incantations and assorted magical actions and proved a complete success – right up to the moment that the Rams played their next game when they duly lost.

INTERNATIONAL SHARP-SHOOTER

Steve Bloomer proved time and again that he knew where the goal was; he was leading scorer for club and country for a considerable time. Although it took him a few games to get into his stride for the Rams, he had no such problems when turning out for England. Bloomer found the back of the net at least once in each of his first ten appearances – his total during that sequence was an impressive 19 goals, and he managed 28 in total for his country in 23 games.

ARCHIE GOES GREEN

An interesting first occurred for Derby County when Archie Goodall received his first call-up to represent his country – he chose to play for Ireland as he had multiple nationality options. Ireland had already reached a half century of fixtures before the Rams man made his debut but he still proved to be the first English Football League player to be capped by them.

RANGERS TURN OUT FOR TED

The largest number of supporters to turn up at Pride Park as fans of the away side is 12,000. The occasion was a benefit match for ex-Derby County favourite Ted McMinn in 2006. The Scottish winger had elicited much sympathy after having to have part of his right leg amputated. A game was arranged between two teams of footballing legends – one representing Derby County and the other Rangers. Because it was felt unnecessary to segregate the crowd as McMinn had been popular north of the border as well as the south, huge numbers of tickets were purchased by Rangers fans. The entire day went off without a hitch.

TEN GREAT HOME MATCHES DERBY 2 SOUTHAMPTON 3

That scoreline doesn't tell the full story as Derby earned themselves a place in the play-off final at Wembley in the most dramatic fashion. Carrying a 2-1 lead from the first leg away to Southampton just three days previously, when Steve Howard had netted both goals, the Rams were – in theory – just 90 minutes away from a crack at promotion to the Premiership having finished third in the regular season.

But, the play-offs were established to create more interest for more teams as the campaign ticks down and once they get underway, they are rarely dull. This encounter was no different, perhaps helped by so many Rams connections in the visitors' ranks; manager George Burley, who had led Derby to the semi-finals two years previously, Inigo Idiakez, that season's Player of the Year, and Grzegorz Rasiak, the leading scorer back then. Play-off football has its own unique atmosphere and just three minutes in Pride Park was rocking as Darren Moore opened the scoring, making it 3-1 on aggregate, although the visitors responded immediately through Jhon Viafara's long-range finish. Eight minutes into the second period, Viafara put Saints ahead on the night and level on aggregate with a powerful strike and by that point, nerves were already being shredded. Enter Giles Barnes just after the hour for an earlier-than-expected return from a knee injury in a move that paid off within four minutes as the teenager forced a corner, then pressured Leon Best to put through his own goal to restore Derby's advantage. Derby got within 90 seconds of the final only to be pegged back by their former favourite Rasiak, such is the nature of play-off football, making it 4-4 and sending the tie to extra-time. There were half-chances at either end but penalties were ultimately required and after four kicks each – with the Rams 4-3 up – Idiakez had to score otherwise it was all over.

The Spaniard had a hit and miss record from the spot with Derby and this time he fell into the miss category, blazing his effort well over the bar and sparking a mass pitch invasion from the fans along with great scenes of jubilation on a night also notable for unseasonably torrential rain. Derby went on to win the final against West Bromwich Albion at Wembley, and many supporters rate that second leg against Southampton as still being Pride Park Stadium's finest hour.

A RECORD LOW

The lowest recorded crowd for a home game played by the Rams dates back to the days before exact figures had to be declared. Attendances were usually estimated to the nearest thousand. This proved to be impossible for the visit of Grimsby Town on April 22nd 1903 as there were simply not enough spectators to reach a thousand. The guess was made at 500, though how such an estimate can be reached remains unknown and although unlikely to be absolutely exact is far enough distanced in terms of size from any others recorded to represent the lowest attendance ever for a Derby County competitive home fixture. The match was not without goals and the record lowest crowd witnessed a 2-2 draw.

RAMS' LINK TO BENFICA

Many Rams fans would have been unaware of the special connection between their team and the Benfica side that travelled to the Baseball Ground for the European Cup match on October 25th 1972. In charge of the legendary Eusebio and co was a man almost as much of a legend himself. His name was Jimmy Hagan. His record as manager of the Portuguese club was impressive as he led them to three consecutive titles. He played some of his early football as a Derby County player himself, but had only 31 games under his belt when he was allowed to move on to Sheffield United. His reward for having his Derby connection was to oversee a 3-0 defeat back on his old turf. Hagan remains, however, the most successful ex-Ram to move into management in club history.

SMITH'S TIME FOR CHANGE

When the time came to remove Jim Smith from the role of manager, his friendship with owner Lionel Pickering proved a stumbling block. The pair had hit it off from the beginning, and though it was becoming obvious that there was a need for change at the club it was a decision Pickering did not want to make. He chose to offer Smith the job of director of football and promote assistant manager Colin Todd to team boss. Despite having been responsible for bringing Todd into the managerial fold at Pride Park his one-time assistant was not keen on having his ex-boss as director of football and the Bald Eagle finished with the club entirely as a result.

WATNEY SETS THE STANDARD

The Watney Cup may have been a small and insignificant trophy in the grand scheme of things, although it does represent the first piece of silverware gained for the team by the managerial duo of Brian Clough and Peter Taylor. Even if the tournament was by invitation only, and the Rams had to overcome only three teams to gain the ultimate prize, a look at the line-up for the final shows how seriously the competition was being taken: Green, Webster, Robson, Durban, McFarland, Mackay, McGovern, Carlin, O'Hare, Hector, Hinton. The crowd took it seriously too, as 32,049 turned out to see Derby win 4-1.

RAMS IN THE CUPS

As well as the three big competitions that the Rams have been regular participants in, the Football League, the FA Cup and the League Cup, there are a number of lesser known ones that they have experienced varying degrees of success in. All the following are considered senior competitions; Watney Cup, Texaco Cup, Associate Members' Cup, Freight Rover Trophy, Full Members' Cup (also known at various times as the Simod Cup, and Zenith Data Systems Cup), Anglo-Italian Cup, and the FA Charity Shield.

FOOTBALL LEAGUE CALLS

Not only have a number of Derby County players represented their country, but a few have represented the Football League in games against other national leagues. John Goodall was the first such representative during the 1890/91 season. In total, there have been 24 players picked for the honour. The full list is as follows: Jack Barker, Harry Bedford, Steve Bloomer, Jack Bowers, Raich Carter, Tommy Cooper, Sammy Crooks, Ron Dix, John Goodall, Kevin Hector, Errington Keen, Leon Leuty, Harry Maskrey, Roy McFarland, Johnny Morris, Bert Mozley, Chick Musson, David Nish, John Robson, Dean Saunders, Peter Shilton, Colin Todd, Ben Warren, and Mark Wright.

MAXWELL ON DOUBLE YELLOW

Only Robert Maxwell could have the front to turn up at the crucial hearing that was hoped would save Derby County and park on double yellow lines in front of the High Court. His offer to the Inland Revenue and the VAT office was to pay 70p in every pound owed. It was declined.

TAX MAN GETS HIS CUT

It is a little known fact that there was a major flaw in the various rescue packages proposed by Stuart Webb and Robert Maxwell when they offered to pay a percentage of what was owed to the Inland Revenue and the VAT office. This was never going to be acceptable to the Football League, even if those offered the deal were prepared to take whatever they could. League rules insisted that all tax bills had to be paid in full. This ruling had been in place for some while and had not been introduced as a response to Derby's offer.

CARTER ALMOST A CROPPER

Raich Carter nearly missed out on taking part in the FA Cup-winning run for the Rams in 1946. The club was only able to register the player for that season's cup competition one hour before the deadline. A missed train connection made for a late-night taxi ride from York to Sunderland for Carter and Derby County club secretary Jack Catterall.

DOHERTY – A BRIEF LEGEND

When supporters talk about all-time greats at the club the name of Peter Doherty invariably comes up. He was a man of great skill and was arguably the greatest player in his position of the era and played an important part in the only FA Cup win to date. His contribution to the Rams' league efforts was considerably smaller, however. He played just 15 league games while at Derby and scored seven goals in the process.

BIG GAME LOW PRICES

The 1946 FA Cup final may have been the biggest game that the country had seen following the end of World War II, but with money in short supply it was not the major earner that it became in later years. The attendance may have been 98,215, but the total value of the ticket sales was only £45,000.

RAMS' WEMBLEY BOW

Although the 1946 FA Cup final was the fourth time that the Rams had reached that stage of the competition, it was their first time at Wembley.

HOW TIMES CHANGE

It has long been argued whether players from the immediate post-war years would be able to hold their own in the modern game. The argument usually suggests that they would, but might struggle to match the fitness level of their modern-day counterparts. There is no doubt that they would find a number of differences in the build-up to games. The post-war squad had regular daily, light training sessions, but by the admissions of the players themselves they frequently had to check the fixture list on a Thursday morning in order to find out who their opponents would be the following Saturday.

A CLEAN SWEEP

The Brian Clough and Peter Taylor revolution was so thorough that when they took over they not only replaced any players that they did not think up to the mark, they also got rid of the chief scout, the secretary, assistant secretary, and the groundsman.

ANYONE FOR TENNIS?

A legendary tennis commentator played a huge, but little known, part in the Rams winning the 1946 FA Cup final. Towards the end of World War II, squadron leader Dan Maskell persuaded Peter Doherty and Raich Carter to become PT instructors at the Medical Rehabilitation Unit at Loughborough College. Furthermore, Maskell brokered a deal with the Rams to provide free tickets for matches in exchange for the services of Carter and Doherty. The pair caught the eye with their displays and were signed permanently by the club.

NOT A SUNDAY BEST

The Rams had to break a 90-year-old tradition on January 27th 1974, with their first competitive match on a Sunday. A major strike involving the power industry had led to three-day working weeks and the prospect of fuel rationing. It was decided as a result to move fixtures to Sundays to help matters and Derby County played a fourth-round FA Cup tie away to Coventry. Both sets of strikers were clearly operating at less than full power themselves as the match ended 0-0. There were objections at the time about using the Sabbath for professional sporting fixtures. Now, of course, they are commonplace.

A WHIRLWIND ARRIVAL

Billy Davies arrived at Derby County in a whirlwind of activity, and not just because of the blades of the helicopter that brought him to his official unveiling. The Scot had been brought to the club as a sign of intent by the new local ownership group after a successful spell as Preston North End boss. Davies quickly went to work revamping the squad. Steve Howard, Stephen Bywater, and Matt Oakley were quickly brought to the club and proved to be the backbone of an ultimately successful promotion push. As with all Davies sides, it took the team a while to hit their stride, but once they got going they started to look unstoppable. Davies always claimed that he and the board of directors had formulated a three-year plan to achieve promotion so it would be unfair to complain about the lack of style in a side which groundout results and found themselves challenging at the top of the table. Both the League and FA Cups proved more than one-round wonders, for a change, though an unexpected defeat away at Plymouth Argyle in the FA Cup was a disappointment. The league juggernaut still rolled on, however, and with further investment during the January transfer window, a top-two finish seemed likely. A late equaliser by Hull City at Pride Park knocked the wind out of everyone's sails and automatic promotion vanished to be replaced by the play-offs. It is a matter of opinion as to whether the Rams were the better of the two sides in either the semi-finals against Southampton, or the final against West Bromwich Albion, but as ever the team dug in and gained victory. Even before the day was over, things started to unravel with comments made by Davies in a post-match interview. The excitement of the day quickly turned to expectation of Premiership football, and Davies spent quite heavily bringing in Claude Davis, Robert Earnshaw, and Kenny Miller for big fees. An exciting opening-day draw at home to Portsmouth, and a narrow defeat away at Manchester City, gave the impression that this might be a decent season, but heavy defeats away at Tottenham Hotspur and Liverpool brought everyone down to earth with a bump. Just one league victory against Newcastle United in the first six matches set alarm bells ringing. A heavy home loss against West Ham United, followed by defeat against Chelsea, set in motion a public falling-out with the chairman, with the inevitable result that Davies left by mutual consent.

BILLY DAVIES WHO ARRIVED AT THE CLUB BY HELICOPTER FOR HIS FIRST DAY AS MANAGER

MISTAKEN IDENTITY

To describe an incident as 'the worst refereeing decision ever' would be impossible. You could fill a book with suggestions and still not reach a definitive conclusion. One of the worst cases of mistaken identity by a match official was witnessed at Pride Park on August 8th 2005. Michael Johnson was spotted by an assistant referee denying a goalscoring opportunity for Brighton & Hove Albion's Colin Kazim-Richards by pulling him back. Referee Martin Harris, however, attempted to red card the wrong central defender – loan signing Andrew Davies. An easy enough mistake to make you might say if it were not for the fact that Davies is blond haired with a pasty white complexion, while the shorter Johnson is clearly from West Indian stock.

CONTROVERSY IN JUVENTUS

There was much controversy surrounding the European Cup semi-final first leg against Juventus in Italy. Assistant manager Peter Taylor had witnessed Helmut Haller, who was on the Juve bench for the game, deep in conversation with the match referee both before the game and again at half-time. Nothing could be proved at the time but an investigation by *The Sunday Times* later proved that the official had been the subject of an illegal approach. He had been offered a sum of $5,000, and a car, if he ensured second-leg victory to the Italians. The referee in question, a Portuguese national called Francisco Lobo, admitted the approach. Lobo, though, was a man of principle and refused the bribe before reporting the matter to Uefa. Those involved in trying to tap him up were suspended 'sine die', however.

LEN GUIDES THE BOARD

Everybody with an interest in Derby County knows that Brian Clough and Peter Taylor replaced the out-of-contract Tim Ward as manager in 1967, but very rarely do the other candidates for the job get a mention. The trio of hopefuls was Alan Ashman, Billy Bingham, and Tommy Cummings. Strictly speaking the three men should not be described as 'the other candidates' for in truth there was a shortlist of three, comprising the names Ashman, Bingham, and Cummings, when ex-professional and newspaper journalist Len Shackleton contacted the Rams' board insisting that they speak to Clough before making a final decision. The rest is history.

BRIAN IN LABOUR

Brian Clough was a lifelong supporter of the Labour Party, a fact which he did nothing to conceal. He was frequently to be found canvassing on behalf of the party at election time. In his time as a striker at Sunderland, he was even invited to become a candidate in the North Yorkshire constituency of Richmond. Given that it was considered one of the safest Tory strongholds in the country it is anyone's guess how he would have done.

MANY HAPPY RETURNS

Some of Derby's greatest players have enjoyed the experience so much that they have returned to the club for a second spell. Whether returning for one last hurrah, or adding genuine contributions to the cause, all were met with goodwill from supporters. A partial list would include; Steve Bloomer, Roger Davies, Bobby Davison, Frank Fielding, Charlie George, Kevin Hector, Roy McFarland and Bruce Rioch.

BOSS GETS HIS WAY

People often state that Brian Clough was prone to overstep the mark at any opportunity. He nearly failed to get the job of Derby manager in the first place thanks to a demand that the board of directors thought preposterous. Not only did he manage to get them to pay him £5,000 per year, but he wanted the club to bankroll an assistant for him. In an era when the role of assistant manager was pretty much unknown, Clough had to make a good case. Whatever he said certainly swayed the directors round to his way of thinking and the Clough-Taylor partnership began to take off in a major way.

NOT FOR THE FAINT-HEARTED

The stress of helping to run Derby County proved so intense for Peter Taylor that he suffered heart problems while in his first spell at the club. It happened twice to him. On the first occasion the Rams were on their way to Highbury when he felt unwell, but he battled through it. The second time was the morning of a home game and Brian Clough arranged for him to see a specialist, who discovered that Taylor had actually experienced a mild heart attack during the first incident.

ROY A TRUE GREAT

Roy McFarland is undoubtedly one of the all-time Derby County greats having made 530 appearances for the club including five from the subs' bench in two spells. He also held the record of most number of England caps while playing for the Rams – until the arrival of Peter Shilton. Even McFarland would hesitate to describe himself as a miracle worker. That is what he would have needed to be to keep the club up in 1984. He did give the team some pride in their performance, however, before handing over to Arthur Cox. He had a better chance to stamp his mark on the side after the departure of Cox some nine years later. Given better players and more of the season to play with, McFarland steered the club to their first-ever play-off final. The Rams had finished in sixth place and faced a daunting two-legged semi-final against Millwall. In a hostile atmosphere, Derby won the away leg and completed the job at the Baseball Ground a few days later. The final against local rivals Leicester City was a disappointment as the Rams lost the game having taken the lead. McFarland's side were slow out of the blocks the following term managing to pick up only one point from the first five games – a start that probably cost them the chance to contest the play-offs two seasons running. It was a season that flickered with promise, rather than ever took off. There were several unbeaten runs when it looked as though the team had hit its stride, most notably a seven-game run that comprised six wins and one draw. It became apparent that the season was going to peter out into mid-table obscurity and Derby missed out on automatic promotion by 13 points. Once it became apparent that another year in the second tier was going to happen, the board of directors decided that there was no future for McFarland whose contract was up at the end of the season anyway. For the directors the decision seemed an easy one to take. McFarland knew before the final home game of the season and said all his goodbyes before a dispirited Derby County team took the field and, unsurprisingly in the circumstances, lost 2-1 to Southend United. The final match of the season was away at Watford. Once again the Rams lost 2-1, but this time with Billy McEwan as caretaker manager.

JOHN A DEAL TOO FAR

John Robertson was the straw that broke the camel's back as far as the friendship between Peter Taylor and Brian Clough was concerned. Cracks had been appearing in the partnership even while the duo were working at Nottingham Forest. A book, *With Clough by Taylor*, was published without the Forest boss knowing anything about it, and having negotiated his friend's retirement package when the assistant-manager decided to retire, was disappointed, to say the least, when his old pal turned up at Derby County a few months later. It was, however, the Scottish winger who put the final nail in the coffin. Robertson's contract was up for renewal and Clough had made several unsuccessful attempts to get the player to commit to a new deal. With the season over Clough went away for a few days and during his absence his former partner struck. The first that the Forest boss knew of the deal was when he made a routine call back home.

BEHIND THE BOARD'S BACK

As the most stylish midfield player of his day, Trevor Brooking seemed a perfect fit for Brian Clough's Derby County. Many supporters thought he would be a great signing and wondered why a deal had never been struck. There are those working for the club who asked the same question. Club secretary Stuart Webb was one of them. Webb was astounded to discover several months after the event in 1972, during a chance conversation with his opposite number at West Ham United, Eddie Chapman, that Clough and Taylor had put in a double bid for Brooking and Bobby Moore for the phenomenal (at the time) sum of £400,000. The bid had been made without mention of it to the Derby board whatsoever.

ANOTHER BATTLE FOR BRIAN

Everyone around at the time knows that the increasingly outspoken Brian Clough was leaving chairman of the day Sam Longson feeling uncomfortable and ultimately led to the showdown and departure of both manager and assistant. It is not so widely known that there had been an earlier argument when one of the directors, Jack Kirkland, told the pair that the club had decided to build a sports complex next door to the ground and money for players was therefore going to be severely curtailed.

PROTESTS BY THE PLAYERS

The departure of Brian Clough and Peter Taylor led to not only protests by supporters, but also a sit-in by the players. With a light on in the boardroom, the players waited outside to confront the board about the decision to accept the resignations of the managerial pair. As it happened, it was only club secretary Stuart Webb and one director, Jack Kirkland. The players gave up and moved off after three hours of waiting, believing that a board meeting was actually being held somewhere else. The only damage done was that to a champagne bucket, which had to be used in an emergency by Kirkland who didn't dare break cover to visit the loo.

LEE LEADS THE WAY

When signing Francis Lee for Derby, manager Dave Mackay explained to the ex-Manchester City striker how important his goals would be on the road if the club was to do well. The Rams boss pointed out how good his men were on their home turf, but said his side did not come up with the goods often enough on the road. Mackay said it was his stated belief that if they could manage six away victories they would win the title. His assessment proved accurate as the Rams won seven times on their travels, and once again won the title.

BLOOMER BEATS LOS BLANCOS

Real Madrid might be giants of the European game, one of world football's true clubs of aristocracy, but the influence of a Derby County legend helped contribute to one of their worst results. Back in May 1924, they reached the final of the King's Cup, in the days before La Liga was formed, and came up against amateur minnows Real Irun. Putting aside the political links – Irun hail from the Basque Country, whose dislike of the capital is well documented – from a footballing point of view the outcome was remarkable as Irun won 1-0. Over Christmas that same year, a pair of friendlies took place between the two teams in Madrid, and ended 3-0 and 7-0. Both to Irun. And there's a strong Derby County connection as the manager of Irun for all three games, who was lauded by the Spanish press for the achievements, was none other than Steve Bloomer.

PAUL PROVES NO JEWELL

Paul Jewell arrived at Derby with a reputation as a manager capable of enabling smaller clubs to run with the big boys. His record with both Bradford City and Wigan Athletic was testament to that. A rumoured friendship with chairman Adam Pearson made for little surprise when the likeable Liverpudlian was brought in as replacement for Billy Davies. Given that the Rams struggled to compete in the top flight from the word go, there was no real pressure on Jewell to save the club from relegation and his mantra from the beginning was that he was building a side to immediately fight for a return to the top flight after the inevitable drop. He almost picked up a point in his first game in charge, away at Sunderland, but was defeated by a stoppage-time winner. He had to wait 11 games to taste his first victory – a win on penalties over Sheffield Wednesday in the FA Cup, but with all the signs pointing to the inevitable return to the Championship, spent a considerable amount of money during the January transfer window. Whether his intention was to make a shot at survival, or give his proposed promotion squad maximum time to bed in together, was never totally clear, as neither scenario panned out successfully. Some of his January signings, like Laurent Robert, were intended as short-term and not very successful, while the arrival of others on more long-term deals fared little better. It took until six games into the following season for Jewell to register his first league win as Derby boss. The victory, a 2-1 win at home to Sheffield United, set Derby off on a six-game unbeaten run and it looked as if a corner had been well and truly turned. Unfortunately, it proved to be something of a false dawn as the Rams quickly lost the consistency that they had shown in that brief spell. The one real highlight of the campaign was the Carling Cup where a run of victories over Lincoln City, Preston North End, Brighton & Hove Albion and Leeds United saw Derby drawn away to Premier League Stoke City in the quarter-final. A coolly taken stoppage-time penalty by Nathan Ellington saw the Rams into the semi-final for the first time in nearly 40 years. Promotion was still the overriding target. December was disastrous with the team managing just four points out of 24. A 1-0 defeat at home to Ipswich Town on December 28th 2008 proved the final straw and Jewell resigned within hours of the game.

ROWLEY'S EIGHT

Steve Bloomer's goalscoring exploits are legendary in their own right but even the Rams' all-time leading scorer never managed something that was once recorded against the club. The date was November 21st 1942, for a game played in the Football League (North) during wartime, with Derby on the road to Wolverhampton Wanderers. And the man in question was Jack Rowley, a Manchester United player by registration who was resident in Ireland but on a fortnight's leave. Rowley agreed to guest for Wolves and went goal crazy, bagging all of the home side's strikes in an 8-1 success. The closest anyone else has ever come to that figure against the Rams is Simon Garner, of Blackburn Rovers, whose five-goal haul in 1983 was enough to secure a 5-1 victory. Even in the disastrous 2007/08 Premier League season the most they conceded to a single player was four, by Chelsea's Frank Lampard in a 6-1 defeat at Stamford Bridge. However, they did concede a few hat-tricks that season, notably to Arsenal's Emmanuel Adebayor, who netted three at both the Emirates and Pride Park to become the first Premier League player to hit home and away hat-tricks against the same opposition in the same season.

SEVEN TOP 500

There are only seven players in Derby County history to top the 500 appearance mark. Incredibly, for a club with over 125 years of competitive football, four of its longest-serving players served under Brian Clough.

Top ten appearances in all competitions:

Kevin Hector	589	1966-77 & 1980/81
Ron Webster	535	1960-78
Roy McFarland	530	1967-81 & 1983/84
Steve Bloomer	525	1892-1906 & 1910-14
Jack Parry	517	1948-67
Jimmy Methven	511	1891-1906
Geoff Barrowcliffe	503	1950-66
Sammy Crooks	445	1927-46
Archie Goodall	423	1889-1903
Steve Powell	420	1972-86

NO LEAGUE TREBLE

By the time April 2011 had been and gone, an amazing FIFTEEN YEARS had passed between Derby County players scoring league hat-tricks! The distinction of being the last man to have done so goes to Paul Simpson, who hit a Division One treble on April 8th 1996 in a 6-2 win for Jim Smith's promotion-chasers at home to Tranmere Rovers. It was the last hat-trick by a Derby player at the Baseball Ground, the venue for so many famous trebles, and in fact no other Ram managed it for almost 11 years in any competition. Arturo Lupoli was the next to bag three, in an FA Cup victory over Wrexham in January 2007, and became the first Derby man to notch a trio at Pride Park stadium. Nathan Ellington then managed the feat in August 2008, in the League Cup against Lincoln City, and in the same competition Tito Villa also hit three at Brighton & Hove Albion a couple of months later. But, in the league the drought was continuing. Only Malcolm Christie and Rob Hulse have genuinely come close; Christie saw a third disallowed in stoppage time of a Premier League thriller with Manchester United in 2002, Hulse scored twice in the Championship against Coventry City in 2009 and then saw a penalty saved.

TOMMY TAKES OVER

There is one noticeable difference between the top-ten list of appearances in all competitions, and those in just league games, as Tommy Powell replaces his son Steve. A sign of the increasing number of competitions the Rams played in the 1970s:

Kevin Hector	486
Jack Parry	483
Geoff Barrowcliffe	475
Steve Bloomer	474
Jimmy Methven	458
Ron Webster	455
Roy McFarland	442
Sammy Crooks	408
Archie Goodall	380
Tommy Powell	380

WORLD CUP RAMS

The pinnacle of football is playing for your country in the World Cup, which took place for the first time in 1930. It wasn't until 48 years later that a serving Derby County player travelled to the finals with his country. Typically, you wait for so long and two come at once in the shape of Bruce Rioch and Don Masson, who lined up for Scotland in the 1978 tournament. Then you've got to look a further 12 years on to find a Ram playing for England in the World Cup, with Mark Wright and Peter Shilton key men in Bobby Robson's side that reached the semi-final in 1990. Five – Igor Stimac, Jacob Laursen, Deon Burton, Darryl Powell and Christian Dailly – went to France 1998, along with Stimac's Croatia colleague Aljosa Asanovic, who had left Derby in the preceding season. It was just one in 2002 in the shape of Branko Strupar with Belgium, though he was joined by former Rams Paulo Wanchope and Mauricio Solis (both Costa Rica), Lee Carsley (Republic of Ireland) and Taribo West (Nigeria), plus future Pride Park men Tomasz Hajto (Poland) and Eddie Lewis (USA). Four years later Wanchope scored the second goal of the tournament, for Costa Rica in the opening game against Germany, and was again in the squad with Solis. Grzegorz Rasiak went with Poland, having joined Tottenham Hotspur in August 2005, while Stern John was in the Trinidad & Tobago squad having taken Rasiak's number nine shirt during a loan spell in the autumn. Lewis again featured for the USA and later played for Derby alongside Mile Sterjovski, who signed in January 2008 having been part of the Australia squad. But in 2010, just one former Pride Park man, midfielder Benny Feilhaber with the USA, made the plane to South Africa. Special mentions go to Algeria's Rafik Djebbour and Australia's Carl Valeri – who both had trials at Derby in 2005 but failed to win deals, only to then go and play in the World Cup.

BLOOMER INSPIRATION DOWN UNDER

The song 'Steve Bloomer's Watching' is well known to all Derby County fans. The same supporters would be amazed if they went to Australia to discover that the song was originally an Australian Rules football song titled 'Up There Cazaly'. The song had been rewritten by two Derby fans in honour of their hero.

JIM'S LEGENDARY ROLE

Jim Smith may well have thought his career in management was over when he accepted a desk job with the League Managers' Association, but a call to take over the hotseat at the Baseball Ground, after predecessor Roy McFarland did not have his contract renewed, led to a period of success that no-one could have anticipated at the time. Smith immediately set about adding to the squad he had inherited and although those he brought in arrived to freshen up the group that was already there his initial batch of Gary Rowett, Darryl Powell, Ron Willems and Robin Van Der Laan all proved good enough for the top flight once they got there. Undoubtedly the best of his initial appointments was Steve McClaren as coach. Much of what the club achieved under Smith can be traced back to McClaren's coaching. The first campaign started poorly with fans looking nervously at the relegation zone after four matches. Things slowly improved thereafter and the signing of the iconic Igor Stimac proved a masterstroke. After losing the first game he played at Tranmere Rovers, the Rams went on a 20-game unbeaten run that propelled them to promotion at the first time of asking. The announcement of the building of Pride Park Stadium came during Smith's first season and although the move to the new ground did not take place until the second Premiership season, there was a feeling of a new era dawning. The first three campaigns in the top flight showed year-on-year improvement and big names such as Stefano Eranio arriving at the club – alongside talented unknowns such as Mart Poom and Paulo Wanchope – saw Derby County finish 12th, ninth, and then eighth before hitting a wall. The following season the Rams escaped the drop by five points and the golden touch in the transfer market appeared to have deserted the Bald Eagle as first the signing of Esteban Fuertes with his forged passport started to unravel, along with the big money purchases of Lee Morris, Branko Strupar, and Georgi Kinkladze, which also failed largely due to a lack of luck where injury was concerned, while the decision to replace future England international Chris Powell at full-back, supposedly because he had gone as far as he could, proved a misjudgement. After the signing of Fabrizio Ravanelli, on terms that Smith disagreed with failed, the team went into terminal decline. Smith was replaced, but his successes should never be forgotten by Rams fans.

PETER'S SECOND COMING

Peter Taylor had been half of the most successful managerial partnership in the history of Derby County, and if his appointment as manager was not met with quite the same enthusiasm as it would have been if Brian Clough was coming back, there was certainly eagerness for the appointment when John Newman needed to be replaced in 1982. If Clough had been the motivator, Taylor had been the talent-spotting half of the duo, a talent that it was quickly proved he retained with the £80,000 capture of Bobby Davison from Halifax. His arrival proved the shot in the arm that the club needed and having only won two games from the start of the season, Taylor's men went on an unbeaten 15-game run in the second half of the campaign. Undoubtedly the highlight of his first season in charge came in early January when the Rams were drawn at home against local rivals Nottingham Forest in the third round of the FA Cup. It was the first time the ex-partners had come up against each other in competition and much was made of the Clough versus Taylor aspect of the match. Against the odds Derby won the game 2-0 with goals from Archie Gemmill, who had been brought back to the club, having spent time away at Forest, and Andy Hill. Another masterstroke from Taylor was bringing Roy McFarland back as his assistant manager from Bradford City. The move once again landed Derby County in trouble with claims of illegal approaches. More controversy followed during the close season as Taylor pinched Nottingham Forest winger John Robertson from under the nose of Brian Clough. There was nothing illegal in what happened, but the matter only served to increase the discord between the two of them. An opening day 5-0 away defeat to Chelsea set the tone for the campaign, and despite the assertions of Taylor that the club would be 'top six by Christmas', victories proved hard to come by. Financial storm clouds continued to gather behind the scenes and although league results proved hard to come by, the Rams embarked on a cup run that took them into the quarter-finals of the FA Cup where they were drawn away to Plymouth Argyle. They drew the match but lost the replay on the very day that a financial rescue package was thrown out of court. After a further financial plan was accepted, Taylor left and went into retirement. This time it was to be for good.

DERBY DUO BRIAN CLOUGH AND PETER TAYLOR ARE IMMORTALISED AT PRIDE PARK

NO VOTE OF CONFIDENCE

When Rams boss Dave Mackay left the club it was as the result of something that he read in a newspaper. He knew that the knives had been out for a while, but the defining moment came when he read of disgruntlement at a successful Midlands club. Realising the implications of the story, Mackay went to the board to seek a vote of confidence. Another Derby County manager was consigned to history within 18 months of winning the title. The club has never been close to it since then.

THE RAMS' GREATEST GOAL

As well as the All-Time XI, supporters were also given the chance to vote for the greatest-ever Derby County goal during the 125-year celebrations. Nominations were narrowed down to a top-ten which would eventually be voted on by the fans to find the top strike. The final vote saw two truly iconic finishes leading the way. The others, in reverse order, are:

10 – Robbie Savage v Doncaster Rovers, free kick in 2009
9 – Dave Mackay v Chelsea, in a 1968 League Cup giant-killing
8 – Trevor Christie v Rotherham United, clinched promotion in 1986
7 – Kris Commons v Nottingham Forest, an FA Cup comeback in 2009
6 – Kris Commons v Manchester United, League Cup semi-final in 2009
5 – John McGovern v Liverpool, won the First Division in 1972
4 – Stephen Pearson v West Bromwich Albion, to win promotion in 2007
3 – Robin van der Laan v Crystal Palace, to win promotion in 1996

None of these goals received over ten per cent of the vote, and in second place with 25 per cent was Charlie George's stunning volley against Real Madrid in a 1975 European Cup 4-1 victory at the Baseball Ground, as part of his hat-trick.

Coming out on top, with 40 per cent, was Paulo Wanchope's amazing effort on his debut in 1997 in the 3-2 Premier League win over Manchester United at Old Trafford, where he took on half of the United side before flicking the ball past Peter Schmeichel from the edge of the box.

TEN GREAT HOME MATCHES DERBY 1 MANCHESTER UNITED 0

There was no other way of summing things up – Derby County were in a bit of a mess when they welcomed Manchester United for the first leg of the League Cup semi-final in 2009. The knock-on of their horrendous season in the Premier League was still being felt, although they had done remarkably well to get this far after seeing off Lincoln City, Preston North End, Brighton & Hove Albion, Leeds United and Premier League side Stoke City. Paul Jewell had recently resigned as manager, then the Rams had scraped past non-leaguers Forest Green Rovers in the FA Cup before announcing that Nigel Clough would be taking over, although not until after the United game. Clough was introduced to the media and the supporters prior to the semi-final but in charge on the night was Academy coach David Lowe. United were massive favourites and included the likes of Nemanja Vidic, Anderson, Nani, Paul Scholes and Carlos Tevez from the start, with Cristiano Ronaldo, Wayne Rooney, Ryan Giggs and Michael Carrick on the bench. The fact that three of those four came on in the second half, including Rooney and Ronaldo just after the hour, showed just what a tremendous performance Derby gave. There had been no sign of the recent turmoil in a passionate opening and Pride Park was on its feet on the half-hour mark with Derby in front. Lowe had given Kris Commons a free role behind Rob Hulse and the midfielder responded with a stunning strike from fully 25 yards that ripped into the back of the net. United were rocked and it wasn't until the second-half introduction of their big guns that they seriously threatened an equaliser with Ronaldo twice going close. Commons, Hulse and Paul Green all went close to putting Derby two up against the defending Premier League and European champions, who had recently added the World Club Cup to their list of honours. But the final whistle blew with Derby 1-0 to the good, an unexpected yet certainly deserved advantage after a great night at Pride Park, and the black and white scarves were waving proudly. Derby travelled to the second leg at Old Trafford just 90 minutes away from their first major final since 1946 but found themselves 3-0 down by half-time, only to rally late on and ultimately go down 4-2 on the night and 4-3 on aggregate in what was only their second-ever semi-final in the League Cup.

HONOURING THE LEGENDS

Along with the votes to decide the All-Time XI and Derby County's greatest goal, the club honoured several legends throughout 2009. The year of the 125th anniversary celebrations kicked off with the unveiling of a striking bronze bust of Steve Bloomer, the Rams' all-time leading goalscorer. The bust sits pitchside at Pride Park Stadium, becoming the first of its kind in the country, and means that – in the words of the song – Steve Bloomer really is watching the Rams. And one of the main men behind the move from the Baseball Ground to Pride Park is also now honoured at the new stadium. Lionel Pickering poured vast amounts of cash into the club to rescue it from the Robert Maxwell era and as chairman he oversaw promotion in 1996 and the change in ground a year later. The iconic directors' entrance from the Baseball Ground was replicated at Pride Park in 2009 and renamed the Lionel Pickering Entrance, a permanent reminder of his service to Derby County. Also throughout 2009, Derby held regular events on matchdays honouring the legends of yesteryear. Reg Harrison and Jimmy Bullions, survivors of the 1946 FA Cup success, were guests of honour at the FA Cup fifth-round match with Manchester United. And at games during the year, the club invited along its legends from different decades to remember the good times they shared. Links to the past continued with the installation at Pride Park of the famous clock, which was formerly housed between the middle and the upper tiers of the Osmaston End at the Baseball Ground. And festivities came to a thrilling close at the end of 2009, with a gala event at Derby's QUAD facility attended by supporters, club officials, legends, and compered by the one and only John Motson. Motson was not chosen purely at random. There is a family connection with the club as his son Frederick is a Rams fan. The young Motson first developed an affinity to the club when his Dad brought some Derby County merchandise back from a game he had been covering.

FROM THE RAMS TO SKY

There are a number of commentators and reporters with affiliations to Derby County, but the most interesting one is probably Rob Palmer who was an apprentice goalkeeper before deciding that reporting on the game – rather than playing it – was the best career move.

DERBY'S TOP SCORERS

The list of top-ten goalscorers in all competitions for the Rams makes for interesting reading, partially at least because of some of the famous names that played for the club who are not on it. It is incredible to note that Steve Bloomer was so prolific in his time at the club that even by adding together the totals of any two of the players below Kevin Hector in the list, it is still not possible to reach Bloomer's total:

Steve Bloomer	332
Kevin Hector	201
Jack Bowers	183
Harry Bedford	126
Jack Stamps	126
Alf Bentley	112
Alan Durban	112
Sammy Crooks	111
Jack Parry	110
Bobby Davison	106

PERSISTENCE FROM HARDY

Although it is common knowledge that Brian Clough was invited to return to Derby County by chairman George Hardy, and which Clough then turned down at the last minute, it is not such common knowledge that Hardy made a further approach of sorts later that same day. While asking the great man why he had changed his mind over the move since speaking the previous day, the chairman offered a sum of £50,000 to be split in whatever way Clough desired between him and Peter Taylor. Clough remained adamant that he was still not coming. In fact, he didn't even mention the offer to Taylor who found out quite by chance some months later.

THE REVOLVING DOOR

When supporters talked of Tommy Docherty's revolving door policy they weren't joking. The Scot was in charge of Derby County for 19 months and either brought in or removed a whopping 40 players in that time. It averaged out at one change every fortnight.

COX A GREAT SERVANT

Arthur Cox was the second-longest-serving manager in Derby County history. Brought to the club by Stuart Webb on the back of a successful spell at Newcastle Cox inherited insufficient players to even field a full 11 all playing in their correct positions. The club had just been relegated to Division Three for the second time in its history. Cox brought in enough players to stabilise the ship but could not get them out of the division at the first time of asking. His second campaign was different as the Rams scraped out of the league in third place, just one point ahead of fourth. Derby went straight through the Second Division and were promoted to the top flight as champions. The astute double signings of Mark Wright and Peter Shilton, who were both full England internationals, bolstered the defence and gave the side a good solid defence to build on, Wright's signing for £760,000 breaking a seven-year transfer record, while the record signing of Dean Saunders, who was the first ever million-pound Derby player, provided the goals necessary to keep heads above water. His team would have qualified for Europe at the end of his second season in Division One if not for English clubs being banned at the time. That was the pinnacle of his time at the Baseball Ground with his side relegated two seasons later. Initially working for the Maxwell family, he found the job increasingly hard as Robert Maxwell changed from being a benefactor giving him money to spend, to a man with business debts forcing the club to sell their assets. He benefited greatly from the arrival of Lionel Pickering as the new owner with money once again available. Cox spent big but was unable to recreate the promotion feats of his early days at the club. He did, however, bring in some decent big-name signings such as Craig Short and Marco Gabbiadini. At the end of his reign, he left with a record of having taken charge of 453 matches, and losing only 108. He was also responsible for taking the club to Wembley for the first time since the 1975 FA Charity Shield as the Rams qualified for the Anglo-Italian Cup final which they lost against Cremonese. Cox eventually found himself incapacitated from doing his job because of a back problem and after a period of suffering called it a day, allowing his assistant, club legend Roy McFarland, to take over the hot seat.

PRIDE PARK WELCOMES THE GREATS

Pride Park Stadium might have only been open since 1997 but the Rams have welcomed some of the game's top names to their current home. Barcelona have visited Pride Park twice for pre-season friendlies, along with other stellar clubs such as Ajax, Lazio and Sampdoria. Serie A giants Sampdoria were the first-ever visitors to Pride Park Stadium for the new ground's opening game in what was a gala occasion. They fielded German legend Jurgen Klinsmann, Argentine midfielder Juan Sebastian Veron, and Italian hot-shot Vincenzo Montella, who had the honour of scoring the first Pride Park goal in a 1-0 win. A year later the giants of Barcelona came to town, starting with the likes of Luis Figo, Luis Enrique and a young Xavi in their team. Paulo Wanchope got one back for the Rams after they went two down but the second-half introduction of World Cup stars Rivaldo, Bolo Zenden and Phillip Cocu helped earn a 3-1 win. CSKA Moscow were the visitors for a 0-0 draw in 1999 before the Spanish flavour returned in 2000 with Athletic Bilbao – featuring Julen Guerrero, Izmael Urzaiz and Joseba Etxeberria in a 2-1 success. Then Barcelona returned 12 months on as Pride Park was packed to see one of European football's most high-profile players, although in a Derby shirt, as Fabrizio Ravanelli made his home debut. Barca stormed into an early three-goal lead with Xavi again pulling the midfield strings. They included Pepe Reina, Michael Reiziger, Phillipe Christanval, Fabio Rochemback, Geovanni and Kluivert, who would all go on to play in the Premier League. In 2002, after relegation from the Premier League, Derby welcomed a second Italian side – Lazio. Fabrizio Ravanelli lined up against his old club, who included Jaap Stam, Fernando Couto, Alessandro Nesta and Hernan Crespo. Adam Murray scored in a 2-1 loss that had plenty of promising signs. It was a double-header for the Rams in 2003 as they first welcomed Dutch giants Ajax – with Wesley Sneijder, Rafael van der Vaart and Jari Litmanen – and earned a 2-2 draw. A few days later, Spanish outfit Real Mallorca came to town with Samuel Eto'o leading their line, though Eto'o was outshone by Izale McLeod in a 3-1 win for the Rams. Espanyol gave Derby a test in a 2-2 draw ahead of the 2007/08 Premier League season and it was Dutch opposition in the shape of FC Utrecht to bring up the curtain on 2008/09 – again finishing 2-2.

COLIN GETS THE CALL

Colin Addison had already built himself a decent reputation as a football manager before getting the call to the Baseball Ground to replace Tommy Docherty after the Scot returned to Queens Park Rangers. The club had escaped relegation to Division Two after flirting with the drop and it was hoped that Addison would be the man to turn things round. It is certainly true that the squad he inherited was considerably weaker than the one taken over by Docherty, but Addison was given money for rebuilding. Barry Powell, Alan Biley and Dave Swindlehurst cost over a million pounds between them but they failed to arrest the decline. Neither Colin Addison, nor his assistant John Newman, had much experience of managing in the top flight, certainly as bosses, but it is arguable whether anyone would have been able to immediately reverse all the damage done by Docherty. It took five games to register the first victory of the campaign, but given that Arsenal were the victims supporters could be forgiven for believing that a corner had been turned. There was, however, no consistency in the side – they only posted back-to-back wins once during the season, and a 4-1 win over high-flying Nottingham Forest, instead of acting as a springboard seemed to accelerate the decline as supporters had to wait a full three months for the next victory. A late rally thanks to the partnership of Biley and Swindlehurst suggested that even though relegation could not be staved off, an imminent return to the top flight seemed likely. In fact 'We'll be back in 81' T-shirts were the must-have item for fans during the summer. As so often at Derby, the promise never fully materialised. Good results were easier to come by in Division Two, but consistency wasn't. Twice they posted three consecutive victories, and once two together, but it was not enough. The Rams ended the season in sixth position in the days before the introduction of the play-offs, and the fact that they ended up 21 points behind champions West Ham United shows how far off the pace they were. The fact that the decline had seemingly been arrested at least enabled Addison to start his third season in charge. The club, though, continued to go backwards and were so inconsistent that between every two wins there was at least one defeat. At no stage did Derby look like taking part in the promotion race. In January the inevitable happened and Addison was dismissed.

OH CANADA

Derby County have signed a number of North American players over the years but Paul Peschisolido remains to date the only Canadian to put on a Rams shirt. The striker was coming to the end of his career when he signed for the club and had already played for a dozen clubs, including loans, but was quickly taken to the hearts of Derby fans. In a career spanning 20 years, Pesch scored 128 goals, including ten for his country, but will probably be remembered by fans at Pride Park for his part in the famous 'coffee cup incident' when Nottingham Forest goalkeeper Barry Roche was beaten as the result of a pass deflecting off a coffee cup on the pitch into the path of the Canadian – allowing him to score.

A BIG SURPRISE FOR JOHN

It is probably fair to say that no-one was more surprised than John Newman himself when he found himself promoted into the managerial hot seat after the departure of Colin Addison. Newman had been an able assistant to the ex-manager but expected to take some of the flak that lack of success had ensured. There was little improvement after the January changeover but Derby did just enough to stay in the division. There may have been several clubs between them and the drop zone, but the most telling statistic was the points tally which showed them to end the campaign just four points better off than the second-bottom club, Wrexham. Scoring goals was not a problem, but keeping them out was, and the Rams conceded 68 – three more than any other team in the division. The following season brought more of the same with the Rams struggling to keep a clean sheet, and at the same time finding it hard to hit the back of the net more than once in each game. In fact they only drew four blanks in the first 16 outings, but only registered one win in the same spell. It was inevitable that something needed to be done and in November, Newman was removed from office. His record showed 25 games in charge and just six wins in total. There were few real highlights during his tenure although the 3-2 win against Watford on the last day of the 1981/82 campaign – when Kevin Hector scored on his final appearance for the club – deserves a mention.

BUILDING THE BASEBALL GROUND

The Baseball Ground was exactly that – a ground for baseball – when Derby County moved there in 1895, having first actually played there in March 1892. Francis Ley laid out a sports ground in the 1880s in order that employees at his Vulcan Works foundry could have recreational facilities. After a visit to the United States in 1889, Ley introduced baseball to the area, hence the name of the ground. Ley, later Sir Francis, had already spent £7,000 to improve the Baseball Ground and added another £500 to extend the football pitch and transfer stands from the County Ground, Derby's former home, upon the club's move. Derby had the chance to move in 1923, to the Municipal Sports Ground on Osmaston Park Road – Moorways as it is more commonly known now – for an annual rent of £500, but broke off talks and in July 1924 paid £10,000 to buy the freehold of the Baseball Ground from Sir Francis Ley. Promotion in 1926 prompted a major redevelopment that saw the B Pavilion erected, with a frontage on Shaftesbury Crescent. Then came an extension to the terracing on the Popular Side, and in 1933 a double-decker stand was opened at the Osmaston End, although Catcher's Corner – part of the old baseball facility – remained in place. Up went the Normanton End in 1935 to bring the capacity to 38,000, less than a decade after the project began. The Osmaston End was damaged in World War II but after it was repaired Derby again could have moved, once more to the Municipal Sports Ground, but the directors rejected the proposal. The first floodlights went up in 1953 but there were then no major changes until 1969, after promotion under Brian Clough and Peter Taylor. Erected was the new Ley Stand, named in recognition of Ley's Malleable Castings, whose factory was behind the new facility. Derby then improved their floodlights in 1972 to meet Uefa regulations after qualifying for the European Cup. But from there it didn't really change until the 1990s and the Taylor Report, which followed the Hillsborough Disaster and meant that grounds needed to be all-seated. The Pop Side terrace was the last to go in 1995, by which point Derby had planned to move and then decided to stay and redevelop the BBG. However, in February 1996 came the announcement that the club would be switching homes to a new site in the city's Pride Park area ready for the 1997/98 season – bringing to an end more than a century of history.

BIG BLUE SHORTS

Football strips, or kits, are described in North American soccer circles as uniforms, with the reason being that apart from the one worn by the goalkeeper, each is exactly the same as the next and they are, therefore, uniform. There is at least one player for Derby County over the years whose matchday outfit was clearly not the same as all of his outfield comrades. That man is David Webb. Webb had played the vast majority of his football for Chelsea but moved to the Baseball Ground at the tail-end of his career, by which time it is fair to say his body had started to fill out a little. As a result his shorts were always a different shade of blue to the others, presumably because the club could find none in his size of the right colour. The different hue of his strip did not deny him the chance to prove that he was still a team player, however, as his wholehearted displays proved.

WORTH EVERY PENNY

Victory over Nottingham Forest has on occasions come at a price, certainly according to various managers. In 2010 it was possible to put an exact figure to that price – £45,000 to be precise. A scuffle between players in the match at the City Ground had ended in unpleasant scenes with players fighting at the end of the game, after what Derby players considered to be provocative over-celebrating by the home team. Both sides were warned as to their future conduct, and when there was similar unpleasantness at the end of the return fixture at Pride Park, there was never any real doubt that fines, or worse, would be brought against both teams. And so it was proved. Allegations from the Forest camp that manager Billy Davies had been kicked up the backside by Rams boss Nigel Clough were subsequently dropped, however.

NEW YEAR CHEER

It was a case of tenth time lucky for the Rams when it came to New Year's Day fixtures. They failed to register a single victory in their first nine attempts but the visit of Fulham on January 1st 1910 provided a 3-1 win and the duck was broken. Horace Barnes, Jimmy Bauchop, and Alf Bentley were the scorers on this historic day.

GOALS GALORE

Derby County fans who followed their side home and away would have seen an incredible goal glut in January 1891. The Rams lost away to Blackburn Rovers by an incredible 8-0 scoreline but rallied ahead of their next game at home to Wolverhampton Wanderers, who they beat by a whopping 9-0.

A RECORD DEFEAT

Scoring two goals away from home – especially in a cup match – is usually a sign of a successful performance. However, the two goals netted by John Goodall counted for nothing when the Rams travelled to Everton for an FA Cup first-round tie on January 18th 1890 as the visitors lost by a massive 11-2 scoreline that remains their record defeat to this day.

HAPPY BIRTHDAY STEVE AND MARCO

Those who believe in astrology and its claims that your character and talents are related to the day and month you are born will argue that proof of their claims exists in the Derby County squad lists as two of the club's star strikers, Steve Bloomer and Marco Gabbiadini, share the same birthday – albeit nearly one hundred years apart.

MCALLE'S GOAL

John McAlle had enjoyed a lengthy career as a central defender, becoming a legend at Wolverhampton Wanderers where he ended his stint there in the top-five list of appearances for the club. He enjoyed a brief spell at Sheffield United but never managed as much as a single league goal with either club. He managed one at Derby, though, in the 3-2 defeat at home to Cardiff City. His final playing record was 482 league games played and one goal scored.

SEVEN SANDWICHED BY WINS

Football has never been an easy game to predict. Take the match against Manchester City on January 29th 1938. Although on a variable run of form, the Rams had the won the game before – 2-0 at Bolton Wanderers – before losing 7-1 at home to City. The Manchester outfit were the first to hit Derby for seven on their own patch – and all this is in a season when they finished second-bottom in the division.

MAXWELL CUTS THE CASH

When the Rams were relegated from the top flight in 1991 their playing record was so miserable that they managed back-to-back victories only four times during the entire campaign. Many of their problems had been caused by owner Robert Maxwell putting the financial squeeze on the club, turning them from a buying club to a selling one.

SHARED LOVE OF KEEPERS

Although there is little love lost between Nottingham Forest and Derby County it is clear that the two clubs share a love of goalkeepers. Since the departure of Brian Clough from the Baseball Ground a number of keepers have turned out for both sides. Both John Middleton and Steve Sutton moved directly to Derby from the City Ground, on two separate occasions in the case of Sutton, both as a loan signing before making his breakthrough to regular custodian of the Forest goalkeeping shirt, and as a permanent signing towards the end of his career. Lee Camp and Peter Shilton have each featured for both teams, but with intermediate clubs in between.

BAMBANG NO DEAL

Derby County, over the years, have been a club of many nations, but have yet to employ any players from Indonesia. The rumour mill started to suggest that things might change during the summer of 2008 as the club were reportedly interested in signing a player from Indonesian side Persija Jakarta. The individual in question was named Bambang Pamungkas. Thankfully, for both chanting supporters and commentators alike, nothing ever came of the story.

BIG-MONEY BAZOOKA

Horacio Angel Carbonari was signed by Jim Smith from Rosario Central and in doing so became the first Argentinean player to turn out for the Rams. Although signed as a defender he managed nine goals in his 90 appearances for the club before falling out of favour. His nickname, which he brought with him from Argentina, was Petaco which means bazooka and came about because of his fearsome shot. Carbonari returned to his first club before injury ended his career and enjoyed a spell there as manager.

TAKING OVER DERBY MIDLAND

Derby County is well known as the city's only professional football club but it wasn't the first big team to be based in Derby. That honour goes to Derby Midland FC, who were formed in 1881 – some three years before Derby County came into being. Midland were founder members of the Midland Football League in 1889 and in that first season they went on to finish second, before finishing fourth the following year. But that second season would prove their last in the competition as they merged with Derby County, giving the town – as it was then – just one professional club. Future Derby County stars Jack Robinson and Steve Bloomer played for Derby Midland, who at least went out with pride by beating County 1-0 in the 1891 Derbyshire Senior Cup final.

STEEL'S TWO RECORDS

It is a rare feat to be able to break the transfer record twice with the same player, but that is what the Rams did with Billy Steel. Derby County paid £15,500 to Morton for him in 1947, breaking the record for players from Scotland, and when they sold him to Dundee for £23,000 three years later broke the record for players moving over the border in the opposite direction. Steel was undoubtedly a talented player but proved a divisive influence while at the Baseball Ground where team-mates often accused him of turning it on only when he could be bothered. The belief was that glamour games in London, or in front of selectors, brought out the best in him, while on other occasions he could not be bothered.

JOHN DELIVERS FOR NIGEL

When Nigel Clough signed John Brayford he was looking for a player who would show consistency in a position that had been up for grabs. The right-back had been a target for an entire season before becoming a Derby player. Brayford himself had hoped to get a number of first-team games under his belt during the 2010/11 season, his first campaign at the club. However, he ended the season having started every single game. He played right across the back four and became the first outfield player to start every game since Andy Comyn in 1991/92. Comyn was also a defender.

ROLLS ROYCE TO DERBY

The city of Derby has long been associated with industry and football. The two big employers in the area have traditionally been British Rail and Rolls-Royce. George Thornewell made the unusual move of signing for the Rams from Rolls-Royce. It proved a good move for all concerned as he made 295 appearances for Derby and won four England caps. He only gained one domestic honour with the club – promotion to the First Division in the 1925/26 campaign.

OPENING CHESTERFIELD'S HOME

Derby County had the privilege of being the first club to play at the b2net Stadium – the new home of Chesterfield. The occasion was a pre-season friendly and although it was the hosts who scored the first goal, the Rams went on to win the match 5-4. The Spireites went on to make the stadium a fortress, losing only four times in the league during their first season. Ironically, Derby played there three times before the end of the 2010/11 campaign, winning each time. They beat Chesterfield in the opening friendly, beat them again in the Derbyshire Senior Challenge Cup, and then beat Buxton in the final of the same competition there.

BY THE FANS

There have been a number of Derby County fanzines over the years. Written by fans of the club, and almost always taking a different view of developments to the official line, they vary from amateurish articles stapled together, to glossy magazines. Derby County has had its share over the years. Some of the fanzines have lasted just a couple of issues while others ran for years. In some cases, the football club was supportive to the extent of stocking issues in their shop, until such time as any perceived negativity was considered too much. It was always accepted that even if critical of the regime of the day, fans wrote the magazines out of a love for the team they supported. The very nature of fanzines means that some rise and fall, without appearing on the radar. The following is as full a list as possible of Derby County themed magazines – *Hey Big Spender, Interesting Very Interesting!, The Sheep, C-Stander, The Mutton Mutineer,* and *We'll Be Back in 81!*

INTELLECTUAL ANDY

It would be both impossible and unfair to single out the most intelligent individual to turn out for the Rams but the name of Andy Comyn would have to be up near the top of the list, if there was one. Comyn was intent on completing his university studies while on the books at Aston Villa. When he arrived at Derby, he may not have become the first player in club history to be the proud holder of a degree in physics, but given that the later stages of his degree course allowed for the study of nuclear and atomic physics there are likely to be few with better credentials. Thankfully, Comyn was purchased for a reasonable price, thus denying pundits the opportunity to say that he cost a bomb.

LESS RUNNING AS A KEEPER

Lee Camp is one of a number of good keepers to appear for the Rams over the years, and one of a smaller breed of goal custodians to come through the ranks and feature for the first team rather than being transferred in. Those who spend their careers diving at the feet of on-rushing forwards often have the reputation of being a little crazy. There was certainly nothing mad about Camp's youthful decision to keep goal, rather than play anywhere else on the park, as when asked why he chose that particular career path he admitted that the decision was made on the basis that there was less running around to do than any position further up the pitch.

BOHINEN MOTORING

Rams boss Jim Smith must have thought he had encountered every type of problem that it was possible for a player to provide him with in his long managerial career. He had, though, never come across an individual like Lars Bohinen prior to the midfielder's transfer to Derby. Bohinen, an articulate and intelligent individual, firstly decided that he would like to learn to be a racing driver during the close season so put his body to all sorts of risks that a footballer shouldn't. Even worse for Smith was the fact that Bohinen had embraced modern technology by creating his own website on which he posted his thoughts on the game and team – whether they were positive or negative.

CAST ADRIFT BY MARINERS

The Rams only lost nine matches out of 46 played in their first campaign in Division Three (North). Unfortunately, two of those games were against table-topping Grimsby Town. If the scorelines had been reversed it would have been Derby County rather than the Mariners who were promoted.

BETTER THAN EVER

In their Division Three (North) promotion season, the Rams went one better – both position and scoring wise – over the previous campaign, finishing top and beating their goalscoring record by one into the bargain. The total of 111 league goals is a Derby County record that is unlikely to be broken.

NO JOY FOR CLOUGH

Middlesbrough equalled the Rams' heaviest home defeat on August 29th 1959 when they registered a score of 7-1. In the Boro line-up was one Brian Clough. The prolific striker netted 251 goals in 274 games throughout his career. Ironically, he failed to manage even one in this match. His career was prematurely ended by injury.

DEBUT FOR WEBSTER

A 2-2 draw away to Bury on March 24th 1962 marked the first appearance of Ron Webster. He was one of the few players to pre-date the arrival of Brian Clough who continued to flourish during the club's greatest period. He was one of very few players to reach the 500 appearance mark, his career total ending with 530 starts and five substitute appearances.

SETH'S GREAT VALUE

The best value for money player ever signed by Derby County has to be Seth Johnson. He may have cost the Rams £3m when signed from Crewe Alexandra, but not only did his transfer to Leeds United net the club a cool £7m, but when he proved surplus to requirements at the Yorkshire club, Derby got him back on a free transfer. He went on to make his final professional appearance in the 2007 play-off victory over West Bromwich Albion at Wembley in a game that was worth £60m to the Pride Park outfit.

WHAT A TRIUMPH

For Ray Straw the 1956/57 season was a personal triumph as he not only equalled the individual goalscoring record for a campaign, he also joined an elite group of players to find the back of the net in six consecutive matches.

POSTER BOYS

Football posters as items for the walls of boys' bedrooms is by no means a modern phenomenon. Although it is virtually impossible to work out exactly when the trend began, it was certainly in vogue by the 1920s. Recently spotted for sale on eBay was a Derby County team photograph originally issued as part of a publication titled Boys Magazine. The magazine was published during the 1925/26 season and was retailing for the princely sum of £30. You never know what it might be worth saving! So better hold on to this book.

THE FIRST PROGRAMME

September 5th 1903 saw the visit of Wolverhampton Wanderers to the Baseball Ground. The match proved to be an unspectacular 2-1 victory for the hosts, but the game deserves a place in Derby County folklore as the first known occasion of the club issuing a match programme to tie in with a game.

A TRAGIC END

Lance Corporal George Brooks suffered the most tragic fate of any Derby County player involved in World War I. He was killed in France a matter of minutes before the Armistice. It is thought he may well have been the last British person killed during the war.

JOBEY ENDS IN DISGRACE

George Jobey was the longest-serving of all Derby County managers. He took charge of the team for 629 games, which currently is more games than anyone in club history. His sides showed more consistency than any until the arrival of Brian Clough. It is unfortunate that Jobey's reign ended in disgrace as a joint commission of the FA and League found both him and the club guilty of a number of illegal payments over a 13-year period.